Healthy Houseplants

Sylvia Woffenden

WITH AN INTRODUCTION BY
Susan Tomnay

BayBooks
An imprint of HarperCollins*Publishers*

A BAY BOOKS PUBLICATION
An imprint of HarperCollinsPublishers

First published in Australia in 1992 by
Bay Books, of CollinsAngus&Robertson Publishers Pty Limited (ACN 009 913 517)
A divison of HarperCollinsPublishers (Australia) Pty Limited

HarperCollinsPublishers (New Zealand) limited
31 View Road, Glenfield, Auckland 10, New Zealand

HarperCollinsPublishers Limited
77-85 Fulham Palace Road, London W6 8JB, United Kingdom

National Library of Australia
Card No & ISBN
186378004 01

The publishers would like to thank the following people and organisations for their
assistance during the production of this book: Lorna Rose for photgraphy on pages
3 and 15; Your Garden magazine for photography of Saxifraga Stolonifara on page 80.

Cover design Elizabeth Seymour
Printed in Singapore by Toppan Printing Co Pty

5 4 3 2 1
95 94 93 92

Choosing indoor plants

The way to choose an indoor plant is to first think of where it's going to go in your house and then choose the plant. If you see a stunning plant in the nursery and bring it home without checking out the room conditions first, chances are you won't have the conditions it needs to thrive and it will die.

First look at your location. Is it sunny? All day sun or for only part of the day? Is it a humid room, getting lots of steam such as a kitchen or bathroom, or is it dry like a living room or bedroom? Do you have room for a pot with a big plant such as a palm or weeping fig, or will your plant be in a small pot on a windowsill or bookshelf? Will it be best as a hanging basket?

If you're starting from scratch and you want to buy a lot of plants, it's a good idea to draw a rough diagram of the relevant rooms - put in doors, windows, heat and light sources and placement of furniture. This way you'll be able to work out the heavy traffic areas, the areas most affected by draughts (which plants hate), the lightest and darkest spots. Once you've done this, you must decide what kind of gardener you are. Are you going to fuss about your plants, watering diligently, wiping over leaves, fertilising regularly? Or do you know from experience that you definitely need easy-care plants? Once you've established all this you can narrow the field of suitable plants.

Displaying indoor plants

Some plants are so striking that they they look best displayed alone. Among these are *Aspidistra elatior*, *Nephrolepis exaltata*, *Ficus lyrata* and *Monstera deliciosa*. But often a collection of plants, both foliage and flowering, grouped together, can make the very best display. Grouping plants will also increase the local humidity so they'll be likely to be healthier in groups than singly.

When grouping plants, try to choose those that require the same amount of water, and of course, they must all require the same conditions for light and temperature.

The plants should all be in individual pots, in case you have to move one or two of them, but aim to place all the pots in a big container perhaps filled with peatmoss or dampened gravel. Or you could arrange them on different levels i.e. some standing on the floor, some in hanging baskets, some on tables, bookshelves etc. You can also display plants on windowsills or on glass shelves in front of a window (only if it doesn't receive direct sunlight) to hide an ugly view.

Containers

One of the mistakes people make with indoor plants is that they put some plants in plastic pots and some in terracotta pots and give them all the same amount of water and fertiliser. Plastic and glazed ceramic pots are waterpoof so the soil will remain moist longer than in terracotta pots which are porous and draw water from the soil. Plants in terracotta pots must be watered much more often than those in plastic or glazed pots, and as frequent watering washes nourishment from the soil, they'll also have to be fed more often.

The advantage of terracotta over plastic, apart from its looks, is that its porous nature allows roots to breathe and it's unlikely that plants in terracotta pots will become waterlogged.

A new pot should be no more than 2 or 3 cm wider than the pot the plant is already in. Many people make the mistake of repotting into a much bigger pot, hoping that they'll never have to repot again. This plan often misfires because the extra soil goes sour before the growing roots penetrate it.

Your pot should be wider at the top than at the bottom. Plants grown in pots that are narrower at the top cannot be repotted without either breaking the pot or damaging the plant's roots.

A pot should have drainage holes, either several small ones or one large one. If you like, place a piece of shadecloth or shard, pinebark or broken crockery over the holes to allow water to drain out and keep the soil in, but this isn't absolutely necessary. A decorative pot can be used as an outer pot with the plant in a pot with drainage holes placed inside.

POTTING SOIL

The ideal potting mix should be a mixture of coarse and fine particles and should feel gritty. It should wet easily but the excess water should drain away quickly leaving the soil moist but not sodden. Try small bags of different kinds of potting mix and test them by allowing a quantity to dry out in a pot. Then try to rewet it.

◆ If it seems to repel water, use a wetting agent. Don't use household detergents as a wetting agent because they can be toxic to plants.
◆ If it becomes soggy, add coarse river sand to make it more porous.
◆ If it is too sandy and doesn't hold moisture, add peatmoss or compost.

Once you've found a mix you like, use it for all your plants.

Unless stated on the pack, potting mixes contain very little in the way of plant food. Mix fertiliser into the soil before you put it into the pots or use liquid or soluble fertiliser, slow-release granules, spikes, pills or mats, applied after the plant is potted up. Don't think that using more fertiliser is going to produce bigger and better flowers or foliage.

PLANTS THAT THRIVE ON NEGLECT

Actually no plant thrives on neglect, but these are not as fussy as some, and if you forget them for a while, the chances are they'll survive.

Aeonium	Mammillaria
Aechmea	Monstera deliciosa
Aloe	Philodendron
Asparagus fern	Plectranthus
Aspidistra elatior	Rhoicissus capensis
Chlorophytum comosum	Sansevieria
Coleus	Saxifraga stolonifera
Crassula	Tradescantia
Dracaena	

PLANTS THAT THRIVE IN SUNNY SPOTS

This is the place for flowering plants. But make sure you don't place your plants too close to the window or they might burn.

Codiaeum	Rhipsalidopsis
Coleus	Sansevieria
Euphorbia pulcherrima	Streptocarpus
Fatsia japonica	

PLANTS FOR DARK PLACES

Nothing actually thrives in dark places, but some plants can liven up a dark corner for a couple of weeks without coming to any harm.

These plants must be regarded as temporary visitors only. If you keep them there too long, they'll die.

Aspidistra	Philodendron
Dieffenbachia	Sansevieria
Fatsia	Syngonium

PLANTS FOR THE BATHROOM

The bathroom is the most humid area in the house, so, as long as you have enough natural light, it's the ideal place (in summer at least) for ferns, palms and other tropical plants.

Adiantum	Aucuba japonica
Alocasia	Begonia
Archontophoenix	Blechnum
Arecastrum romanzoffium	Caladium
Asplenium	Calathea
Athyrium australe	Caryota

Chamaedorea	Leea coccinea
Clerodendron thomsonae	Licuala spinosa
Codiaeum variegatum	Livistona australa
Coleus blumei	Monstera deliciosa
Columnea	Nematanthus longipes
Crossandra	Neoregelia carolinae
infundibuliformis	Nephrolepis exaltata
Ctenanthe	Pellionia
Cymbidium	Peperomia
Cyperus	Pilea
Cyrtomium falcatum	Plectranthus
Dichorisandra reginae	Polyscias balfouriana
Dieffenbachia	Rhapis excelsa
Dizygotheca elegantissima	Rhoeo spathacea
Dracaena	Ruellia makoyana
Episcia dianthiflora	Saintpaulia
Fatsia japonica	Scindapsus aureus
Ficus	Selaginella
Fittonia verschaffeltii	Spathiphyllum
Gynura sarmentosa	Streptocarpus
Hypocyrta	Vriesea splendens
Hypoestes sanguinolenta	

PLANTS FOR THE KITCHEN

Plants in the kitchen have to put up with heat, steam and sometimes smoke, so they need to be fairly hardy. As long as the kitchen is brightly lit, the plants listed above as suitable for the bathroom, will also do well in the kitchen. The following are plants that thrive in humidity.

Caladium	Dieffenbachia
Columnea	Neoregelia carolinae

PLANTS FOR HOT DRY ROOMS

Cactuses and succulents thrive in hot, dry conditions, but they need plenty of light. Cactuses look particularly appealing when you group them in a shallow dish.

Aeonium	Mammillaria bocasana
Aloe	Pteris
Aporocactus flagelliformis	Schlumbergera
Chamaecereus sylvestri	Sedum
Crassula	Zygocactus
Echeveria	

REPOTTING

1 CAREFULLY REMOVE POT-BOUND PLANT

2 PLACE GRAVEL OR BROKEN POT AND A LAYER OF SOIL IN NEW POT BEFORE SETTING PLANT

3 ADD ENOUGH FRESH SOIL TO REACH 2-3 CM BELOW RIM AND PRESS DOWN FIRMLY

4 WATER THOROUGHLY AND ALLOW TO DRAIN

WHEN TO REPOT

The first symptoms of a pot-bound plant are:

◆ stem and leaf growth is very slow even when the plant is fed regularly in spring and summer
◆ the soil dries out quickly and you have to water much more frequently than usual
◆ you see roots growing out of the drainage holes

As a final check, invert the pot onto your open hand with the stem between the middle fingers. If the plant doesn't slide out easily, put a finger into the drainage hole and push, or lightly tap the rim of the inverted pot on the edge of a bench. If the soil ball is white with roots, it is time to repot. Plants that have not filled their present container with roots do not need repotting. Just replace the plant and soil in the pot and no harm will have been done.

Light

All indoor plants need some light, most need quite a lot. The area in front of a window is the brightest part of any room and the best place for your plants. However, the light will vary, depending upon the direction that the window faces. Rooms with north-facing windows are the brightest, south-facing windows are the dimmest and east- and west-facing somewhere in between. Naturally light will be reduced if there are trees or buldings obstructing the sunlight for all or part of the day.

So if you have a room with a large north-facing window that gets sun all day, is this the perfect spot for plants? No, it will almost certainly be too hot for most plants (with the exception of cactuses or succulents) unless you move them

HOW TO REPOT

Make sure the pot you're transplanting into is absolutely clean. If it's been used before, scrub it out with hot water and a stiff brush, so that there's no chance that any diseases or pests that might have been in the soil will live on. Cover the drainage holes with shadecloth, pinebark etc., and remove the plant from the old pot as described above. If it's a big pot, you'll probably need help since you won't be able to invert the pot and remove the plant by yourself.

Measure the soil ball to make sure it will not be too high or too low in the new pot. Allow for a 2 cm space between the top of the pot and the soil surface. Add to or remove soil from the pot before you set the plant into it.

Stand the plant in the new pot, holding it steady with one hand while you add soil with the other. Firm the soil down as you go. When it's finished, water it thoroughly and allow it to drain, then place it in indirect light for at least two weeks to help it recover from the shock of transplanting and then put it in its permanent position. Overdosing with fertiliser is a sure way to set back or even kill plants.

after they've had a couple of hours of early morning sun. To make the area in front of the window a plant haven, hang gauzy curtains to filter the light.

You can safely place plants in front of the window in dimmer rooms and always rotate plants from dim corners to lighter areas at least every two weeks. But never place a plant that has been growing in a dim room into direct sunlight or it will be seriously burned within a couple of hours.

A plant growing in front of a window should be turned daily to keep it symmetrical in shape, because it will naturally grow towards the light.

If you don't have enough natural light to grow plants indoors, you can grow them under artificial light. Install fluorescent lights under a shelf or cupboard and position the plants underneath. The lights are left on for 14 to 16 hours each day. Plants grow well under lights but they must be kept pruned so that they don't get too close to the lights. They have to be about 90 cm from the light source to get any benefit.

Room temperature

Most indoor plants are tropical, and they don't fare too well in the cold. When the temperature in your house drops below 10 degrees you have to expect some plant deterioration. The colder your house gets at night, the more likely your plants are to suffer. Unless you keep the house heated night and day there's little you can do about it. But you can minimise the damage by making sure that you don't place plants close to heaters. They would rather be cold all the time than alternately hot and cold. As well, keep them out of draughts - breezy corridors, open windows, fans and airconditioning outlets. Never leave pots between the windows and drawn curtains on a cold night because this is one of the coldest places in the house.

Excessive summer heat won't affect your tropical plants as long as you keep them moist and humid by misting them several times a day or, in really hot weather, grouping your plants together on a tray of pebbles which are not quite covered with water.

Another way to add humidity is to put the plant in a porous pot inside a large non-porous container, filling the space between them with moisture-holding material such as damp peat, sphagnum moss or even newspaper. This is known as double potting and is particularly effective for ferns.

Feeding

All plants require certain mineral and trace elements to grow. Three elements, nitrogen (N), phosphorus (P) and potassium (K) are needed in larger quantities than others.

Don't overfeed. More plants are killed by excess fertiliser than die from not enough. Start to fertilise your plants when the weather begins to warm up in spring, and keep fertilising until the first chilly days of autumn. During the cold weather plants tend to stop growing and need no fertiliser at all.

There are many fertilisers to choose from - liquid or soluble fertilisers whose dosage should be followed exactly and slow-release fertilisers which offer continuous feeding over a certain period. These come in granules, spikes, pills or mats. Make sure you note the date of application so that you'll know when to replace them.

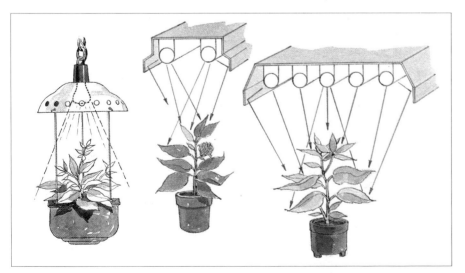

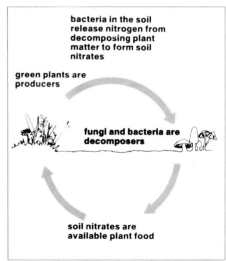

INCANDESCENT PLANT LIGHTS (LEFT) AND FLUORESCENT TUBES (CENTRE AND RIGHT) MAKE IT POSSIBLE TO GROW INDOOR PLANTS WITHOUT SUNLIGHT. MAKE SURE THE LIGHT REACHES ALL THE FOLIAGE, OR PARTS OF THE PLANT WILL LOSE COLOUR OR DIE

Watering

The golden rule for watering plants is that when you do water them, water them deeply. Little and often is not the way to go with plants - their roots will stay close to the surface and they won't thrive. But don't let your plants stand in a saucer of water over a long period.

As to how much water, it depends upon a number of factors.
SOIL ABSORBENCY Rich peaty soil will hold more water than sandy soil and so needs to be watered less often. Pot size. Generally big pots need water less often than small ones, because the soil dries out quickly in small pots.

Air temperature and humidity. When it's hot and dry in the house your plants will need more water than in cool moist weather.
INTENSITY OF LIGHT Plants in bright light need more water than those in a darker spot.

The size of the plant. Big plants use more water than small ones.
THE NATIVE HABITAT OF THE PLANT Tropical plants (i.e. most indoor plants) need a lot more water than those from dry, arid areas. Some plants like to be keep continually moist while some like to dry out between waterings.

Most plants should be keep drier in winter than in summer (unless your house is heated all the time and very dry). A useful tool to assess soil moisture level is a plant-prober which, when pushed into the potting soil, changes colour according to the moisture content. However your finger works just as well. Push it into the soil to a depth of about 3 cm. You do this because sometimes the topsoil is dry while underneath it's quite moist.

If the potting mix has shrunk away from the sides of the container, it is close to drying out completely and any water poured onto the top will run down the sides and out of the drainage holes. In this case submerge the pot in a bucket or sink of water until all the air bubbles have been forced out. Test for moistness with your finger, and drain the pot before putting it back in its saucer.

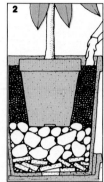

METHODS OF WATERING INDOOR PLANTS
1 MIST-SPRAYING
2 DOUBLE POTTING
3 ALLOWING PLANT TO ABSORB WATER FROM A DEEP SAUCER
4 CREATING A HUMID ATMOSPHERE BY STANDING THE POT ON PEBBLES IN A LARGE DISH FULL OF WATER

Below ◆ KEEP THE LEAVES OF TROPICAL PLANTS HEALTHY BY WIPING WITH A DAMP CLOTH AND MIST-SPRAYING

Below Right ◆ MOST PLANTS PREFER TO DRAW UP WATER FROM BELOW (RIGHT) OR TO ABSORB WATER THROUGH A POROUS POT (LEFT)

Right ◆ SUN, AIR AND MOISTURE ARE ABSORBED THROUGH THE LEAVES; MINERALS AND WATER THROUGH THE ROOTS

What's wrong with my plant?

A sick houseplant is a miserable sight. The easiest problems to identify are those caused by insect infestation, but most houseplant ailments stem from their environment: too much or too little water, light, fertiliser, humidity or heat. These are much harder to diagnose correctly. You can minimise the risk of plant ailments.

◆ Keep your plants clean. Plants not only look better if their leaves are free from dust, but they breathe better too. Use a moistened cloth and support the underside of the leaf with one hand while you wipe it clean with the other. Hairy-leaved plants, such as African violets, can be cleaned with a fine, soft brush.

◆ Check your plants regularly, daily if possible. Feel their soil for moisture, check both sides of the leaves and all stems. Look for anything unusual — brown leaf tips or edges, spotting or mottling, wilting, webbing in the leaf junctions, yellowing leaves, spindly growth, smaller than usual leaves and any kind of creature, active or immobile.

RED SPIDER MITES

These are the indoor gardener's biggest enemy. They're tiny insects which suck sap from the underside of leaves, causing, at first, a fine yellow mottling to appear on the upper sufaces. In time these merge and take on a silvery sheen. Very fine webbing is usually obvious at leaf junctions. Spider mites thrive in dry air, so daily misting of both sides of the leaves will help discourage them. Infested plants should be taken outside and sprayed thoroughly with a miticide. Or you can swish the foliage of an upended plant through a sudsy mix of mild soap (not detergent) and warm water - but make sure you cover the soil with foil to stop it spilling out. Repeat this weekly until pests are gone. Once you find red spider mites on a plant, check all your other plants for infestation.

MEALYBUGS

These are white, cottony blobs that live under leaves and in leaf junctions. Dab each with a cotton bud dipped in methylated spirits or spray the plant outside with a suitable insecticide.

SCALE

These are immobile little ovals which attach themselves to stems or leaves and can spread quickly into a serious outbreak. Scrape off minor outbreaks with your fingernails or spray the plant with a suitable insecticide.

APHIDS

Green or black pests that cluster in colonies around flower buds, on new growth or under leaves. Control with a soapy water wash or treat with a houseplant spray.

HERE ARE SOME TYPICAL PLANT PROBLEMS AND THEIR SOLUTIONS.

SYMPTOM	CAUSE	CURE
Leaf tips turn brown, lower leaves turn yellow than fall off. Stems may be soft, mushy and brown. Soil is soggy.	Too much water.	Allow soil to dry out completely before rewatering, then water only when the soil feels dryish. Repot into sandier soil if drainage is inadequate.
Leaf tips turn yellow, then brown and crips. Lower leaves turn yellow. Plant looks dull and wilted.	Too little water.	Immerse pot in sink full of water until bubbling stops. Drain then water whenever the top 2 cm of soil feels dryish.
Leaves look faded or have yellow or brown 'burned' spots.	Too much light, probably direct sunlight.	Move plant out of direct sunlight but not into a very dim spot.
Long, spindly stems, excessive distance between leaves. New growth weak, pale and smaller than usual.	Too little light.	Move to brighter light but not direct sunlight. Trim spindly growth to encourage bushiness.
Growth is fast but weak. Stems are spindly and leaves may be streaked with yellow. White crust may appear on soil surface or pot sides.	Too much fertiliser	Either repot into fresh, well-drained soil (shaking off as much of the old soil as possible) or wash out the excess fertiliser by watering the plant several times an hour with tepid water. Don't feed again for a while and when you do, reduce the dosage.
Leaves turn yellow but veins are green. New growth is weak and droopy.	Too little fertiliser.	Feed with fertiliser suitable for indoor plants, following directions on the pack. Do not use more than specified.
Leaf edges curl under, turn crisp and brown.	Too little humidity or too hot or both.	Mist leaves with hand-held atomiser at least once a day. If too hot, move to a cooler, bright room.
Whole plant droops.	Too cold or draughty.	Move to a warmer, well-ventilated room without any draughts.

Holiday care

WINTER HOLIDAYS: Don't leave your plants on windowsills as this is the coldest place in the house. Place them all together in a tray or trays in a bright room and water them thoroughly. Surround them with damp peatmoss or place them on a bed of pebbles not quite covered with water. This is to produce a humid atmosphere.

SUMMER HOLIDAYS: A plant is actively growing in summer and so needs much more care and attention than in winter. If you're going away for more than a week in summer your best bet is to get a friend to call in and look after your plants. But bear in mind that your precious plants aren't as precious to someone else and that not everyone has green fingers. To make the job easier for your plant minder:

◆ Put all your plants in one place. The perfect spot is a shady area in the garden that is sheltered from the wind and never receives full sun. The plants will benefit from the fresh air and rain and can be watered with the hose. If this is not possible, the best places in the house are the bath, bathroom floor, laundry tub or kitchen sink.
◆ Group your plants according to how much water they need and leave notes with instructions on watering.
◆ Don't ask your minder to feed the plants - unless you're going to be away for months.
◆ Don't draw the curtains in the rooms containing the plants. They must have plenty of bright light, but not direct sunlight.
◆ If it's at all possible to safely leave a window open, do so. Plants need ventilation.

If you can't get a plant minder, there are several alternatives, their success depending upon the length of time you'll be away.

In all cases, trim off the flowers and flower buds. You won't be there to enjoy them and blooming weakens plants on minimum care.

UP TO TWO WEEKS ABSENCE This method works for plants in terracotta pots. Place the pots into a larger pot that has a thick layer of sphagnum moss in the bottom of it. Push additional moss down the sides of the holding pot until it is full. Water the plant and moss thoroughly and place in a cool but bright room, out of direct sunlight.

MORE THAN TWO WEEKS ABSENCE
1. *The bathroom greenhouse* This method only works if you have a bathroom that gets lots of light.

◆ Put the plug in the bath and line it with plastic sheeting.
◆ Put a layer of newspapers at least 3 cm thick in the bath and turn on the tap. Leave the newspaper to soak until it is really sodden, then drain off the remaining water.

◆ Water the plants well and place them, without their saucers, on the newspaper in the bath. If the plants don't rise above the top of the bath, place a sheet of clear plastic over them and tape it to the bath. Smaller collections of plants can be housed in the same way in laundry tubs or the kitchen sink.

If the plants are too tall to cover with plastic, fill the handbasin with water and leave bowls of water on the windowsill for additional humidity. Close the door.

2. *Individual greenhouses* This method involves wrapping individual plants, pots and all, in clear plastic. It gives the plants a warm, humid atmosphere and prevents them from drying out.

You'll need lightweight, clear plastic bags (dry cleaning bags are perfect) and slim bamboo stakes. Several small plants can be put in one bag, but larger speciments will need their own individual 'greenhouse'.

◆ Push three or four bamboo stakes into the soil around the edge of the pot. The stakes must be taller than the plant, to keep the bag off the leaves.
◆ Water the plant thoroughly, but take care not to wet the foliage; too much moisture inside the bag could encourage fungal diseases.
◆ Slip the bag over the stakes and tape to the bottom of the pot.
◆ If you have a plant that is too big to bag, then enclose only the pot and tie the bag firmly around the stem.

3. *Water wicks* Use lamp wicks (you can buy them at hardware stores or camping shops) to transport water from a reservoir to the plant roots.

◆ Gently up-end the plant and tap the pot so the root mass comes out intact.
◆ Thread a length of lamp wick through the drainage hole and coil it around the bottom of the pot once or twice.
◆ Replace the plant in the pot and water well.
◆ Stand the pot on a couple of bricks in a container of water. Be sure that the pot is clear of the water but that the wick is right down in the bottom of the bowl and is well submerged.

COMING HOME FROM HOLIDAYS Don't immediately remove your plants from their plastic bags or humid bathroom. The shock of moving them to their usual position could set them back and all your holiday care will have been for nothing. Instead get them used to drier conditions gradually and make sure you mist the leaves daily.

Pruning

The purpose of pruning is to shape the plant attractively and also to direct the growth habit. You should only prune when the plant is well-rooted and actively growing. Some houseplants will never need pruning; being contained in a pot automatically restricts their size.

The two ways of pruning pot plants are pinching and cutting back.

Plants such as coleus, which should be bushy, need side shoots. To achieve this, pinch out the tender growing tips, i.e. the top 6-12 mm of the stems. Pinching will also encourage more flowers on some plants. For a really bushy growth, the resultant side shoots can also be pinched out when they are about 8 cm long. Climbing plants require long, trailing stems so one or more strong main shoots should be selected and trained as required, the weak side shoots being cut back cleanly at their junction with the trained stems. Do this in spring. Soft-stemmed plants can be pruned with a really sharp gardening knife or razor blade. Plants with tougher stems should be pruned with a pair of secateurs. Generally, only lightweight secateurs are ever needed for houseplants.

Plants such as *Monstera*, which have a tendency to grow too large for your room, should be cut back in spring to a point just above a leaf. While some flowering plants bear their blooms on new growth and need to be pruned at the end of the flowering season, others, such as Hoya, flower on previous growth and should not be pruned.

Always cut out dead and diseased stems and remove dead flowers and leaves.

Supporting climbing plants

If you don't support some climbing plants you'll end up with trailing plants. In some cases this is desirable and they can, look wonderful in hanging baskets. But tall, straight-stemmed plants, if not supported, will develop kinks and bends and can look most unattractive.

When deciding upon the kind of support your plants need, try to estimate the height they are likely to grow to. While some supports can be removed and replaced while the plant is growing, it is difficult to remove supports such as moss poles once the plant has rooted in the moss.

MOSS POLES These are mostly used for climbing plants that produce aerial roots from their stems, for example, *Monstera deliciosa*, *Philodendron* and *Scindapsus aureus*. Provided the moss is kept moist, the roots will penetrate into it and thereby support itself. You can buy moss poles from nurseries.

WIRE NETTING CYLINDER A cylinder of small-mesh wire netting, about half the diameter of a large pot, can make a good support for ivy. Place the cylinder in the centre of the pot and plant three or four young ivies around it. They will cling to it and soon grow into a thick column of foliage. You may need to place a couple of bamboo canes inside the cylinder for support.

WIRE HOOPS These are good supports for some flowering climbers such as *Hoya carnosa*, which flower more freely if their stems are trained in circular fashion rather than straight up.

TRELLIS You can buy pots which include a ready-made trellis or you can make your own trellis with bamboo canes tied together with twine. This make good supports for *Cissus*, *Asparagus* and ivies.

BAMBOO CANE This is the simplest of all supports. Use a thick cane to support tall, straight-stemmed plants such as *Ficus lyrata*, and thin split canes for supporting very samll plants. For plants with large flowering heads such as *Hyacinthus*, a split cane should be placed just behind each stem.

TYING IN Use soft green garden string, fine plastic coated wire or raffia to tie your plants to their support. Never tie in stems tightly - they must have room to thicken. A tight cane can kink or cut into the stem, and can even kill off the part of the stem above the knot.

Propagation

You can grow indoor plants from seeds, cuttings (leaf or stem), and air-layering.

CUTTINGS

This is the easiest way to propagate and it means that you can increase the number of your own favourite plants, or you can take cuttings from a friend's healthy plants.

◆ Make sure the plant you intend to take a cutting from is perfectly healthy. Remember, a cutting is a clone — whatever qualities the parent plant has, including diseases, will be passed on.

◆ Choose a stem that doesn't have any flowers or flower buds and cut it off, with a sharp knife or secateurs, about 7-10 cm from the top. Make the cut just below the bulge where the leaf joins the stem — this is called the node. Remove the lowest pair of leaves.

◆ Dip the cut end into some hormone rooting powder and shake off surplus. This contains growth hormones that encourage a cut shoot to grow strong healthy roots.

◆ Place the cuttings in small pots in a mixture of moist peatmoss and horticultural sand.

◆ Make holes first with a pencil so that you're not forcing the stem into the soil. Water thoroughly.

◆ Place short split canes in the pot and cover the whole thing with a plastic bag, making sure the bag doesn't touch the foliage.

◆ Place the pot in a warm spot in good light, but not direct sunlight. Usually there is enough water in the soil to last until the plants have rooted. You can tell when your cuttings have rooted by new leaf growth. Leave them in the pot for about two weeks after you have first spotted new leaves, taking the plastic off the pot for longer and longer periods each day. Once the new leaves are looking healthy and strong, pull out the plants and check their roots.

◆ Plant each rooted cutting in a small pot. Young plants grow best when their roots don't have too much room to explore.

◆ Some cuttings will root in water. Prepare cuttings in the same way as described above. Use a jam jar with about 25 mm water in the bottom and stretch a piece of plastic wrap across the top. Make holes with a sharp pencil to hold the cuttings. Push each cutting carefully through its hole so that the bottom of the stem just enters the water. Put the pot in a warm, bright place, but not in direct sunlight and inspect daily to see if the roots are growing. This method will work with *Tradescantia*, *Zabrina pendula*, *Coleus blumei* and *Codiaeum variegatum*.

LEAF CUTTINGS

Some plants can be propagated from their leaves, some from leaf sections. Each leaf or leaf section will produce several new plants so it's a very economical way to grow indoor plants.

USING LEAVES WITH STALKS

This method is suitable for *Saintpaulia*, *Peperomia argyreia*, *Begonia bowerii* and *Sinningia speciosa*.

◆ Slice a leaf from the plant, together with 13-25 mm of stalk, using a razor blade or a very sharp knife. Dip the end of the stalk into a hormone rooting powder and insert the stem into a shallow tray of seed and cutting compost. Water them in.

◆ Cover the tray with plastic wrap or a sheet of glass and leave in a warm, light room out of direct sunlight. They will root in about six weeks; shoots will appear in about ten weeks.

◆ When the plantlets are about 2.5 cm tall, split up the clusters and pot them into individual pots filled with a peat-based compost. Grow them in bright light but not direct sunlight and feed them every second watering with a fertiliser high in phosphate and potassium, but low in nitrogen - a tomato fertiliser is ideal.

USING WHOLE LEAVES

Suitable for *Begonia rex*, *B. masoniana*, *Crassula*, *Echeveria* and *Sedum*.

◆ For the succulents (*Crassula*, *Echeveria* and *Sedum*) slice a leaf off the stem and allow the gummy sap to dry for a day or two.

◆ Insert them up to a quarter of their length in the tray of compost and water them in. Cover the tray with plastic wrap or glass, making sure it doesn't touch the leaves and rooting will start within two to three weeks.

◆ For *Begonias*, slice off a whole leaf and lay it on a flat surface with the underside facing up. With a razor blade, make cuts through each vein where it joins with another - you'll have half a dozen or more cuts, depending on the size of the leaf.

◆ Water the prepared compost so that its surface is slightly damp, and lay the leaf, cut side down, flat on top of the compost, anchoring it firmly in place with one or two pins. Water it in and cover the tray with plastic wrap or glass. Keep in a bright position, out of direct sunlight. Plantlets will begin to form from each of the cut veins after five to six weeks.

USING LEAF SECTIONS

You can make even more plants from *Begonia rex*, *Sanseviera* and *Streptocarpus* by cutting one leaf into several smaller sections. You'll get several new plantlets from each section.

◆ Choose a big leaf and cut it into 2.5 cm squares. This will automatically make the necessary cuts through the veins. You then lay each section flat on the compost as for whole leaves or, in the case of *Begonia masoniana*, *Sansevieria*, *Streptocarpus* and *Sinningia speciosa*, insert each section upright in the compost to about half its length, as you would when using leaves with stems attached. Make sure that the biggest

severed vein in each section is inserted in the compost.

◆ Water well, cover with plastic wrap or a sheet of glass and place in a bright room out of direct sunlight.

AIR-LAYERING

This is an excellent method of propogating stiff-stemmed plants which, when they grow too big for your living room, can be started off again as pretty small plants. Air-layering should be done in late spring or early summer.

It is suitable for *Ficus*, *Dieffenbachia* and *Monstera deliciosa*.

◆ Soak some sphagnum moss in water overnight. The next day select the stem you've chosen for air-layering. It can be the main stem or a strong side shoot.

◆ About 15-30 cm from the top of the plant, cut away a few leaves to give you some space and, using a very sharp knife, make a slanting upward cut about 5-7 cm long but not penetrating more than half way through the stem.

◆ Coat the wound with a hormone rooting powder and pack it with a small, moist wad of sphagnum moss.

◆ Take a couple of handfuls of moss and squeeze out the excess water. Work it into a ball, divide it in half and press half into either side of the stem where the wound is. Squeeze the moss gently together and secure it around the stem with thread or sticky tape.

◆ Wrap the wound securely with plastic wrap and seal it, top and bottom with waterproof adhesive tape.

◆ Keep the plant in a warm, humid atmosphere and mist it daily with a hand-held atomiser.

◆ White roots will start to appear in about eight weeks. When you see them, remove the plastic bandage. Make sure you have a pot ready to take the new plant. Fill it with potting mixture.

◆ Make a horizontal cut just below the ball of moss, clear of the roots and immediately place the stem, moss and all, into the potting mix. Do this carefully since the roots are brittle. Water the plant well.

SEEDS

The easiest plants to grow from seed are *Asparagus*, *Coleus blumei*, *Philodendron* and *Hypoestes sanguinolenta*.

◆ If you have a lot of seeds, use a shallow tray rather than a pot. Use a seed compost and fill the tray to within 13 mm of the top. Level and smooth the soil with a flat piece of wood.

◆ Space out large seeds individually, roughly 13 mm apart, across the compost surface. Sprinkle smaller seeds evenly over the surface. Tiny seeds should be mixed with fine sand before sowing.

◆ Cover the seeds with fine layer of compost and water them in using a fine mist sprayer to avoid unsettling them.

◆ Cover the tray with plastic wrap or put the whole tray into a plastic bag and place in a light position, out of direct sunlight.

◆ Mist-spray the compost whenever it looks as if it might dry out.

◆ The time it takes for plants to germinate varies enormously. Some plants take only a week or two, but palms can take six months or more.

◆ As soon as seedlings appear, make sure they are in good light, but out of direct sunlight. If the light is poor the seedlings will be spindly.

◆ If you have planted too many seeds for the tray, thin out the seedlings, choosing the weakest looking ones.

◆ Once the seedlings start to look strong, transplant to individual pots of compost and keep well watered, but not soggy.

Seasonal care

WHAT TO DO IN SPRING

Once you see new leaves and shoots on your plants you know that spring has arrived for them, even it it's not official yet.

◆ Now's the time to gradually increase their water intake and to start feeding them after their winter break. When watering, allow the plant to dry out before you water it again. This will be your best indicator of how much water it needs. Overwatering and overfeeding usually occur in spring, when the plant owner gets over enthusiastic.
◆ Once plants have started into active growth you can repot them if they need it. Be careful not to over-fertilise plants when they're just beginning to grow again.
◆ Include your plants in your spring clean. Wipe their leaves and trim and prune where necessary.
◆ Pests will start showing themselves in this season. Watch out for aphids on any new shoots and flower buds; red spider mites on the underside of leaves; mealy bugs on the undersides of leaves and in the leaf axils; and scale insects on leaf stems and veins.

As soon as you have identified the problem, take immediate action, or it could become much more difficult to deal with later on.

WHAT TO DO IN SUMMER

Summer is the active growing time for most indoor plants, the time when they need the most watering and feeding.

◆ Never just water your plants willy-nilly, thinking that because it's summer they must need plenty of water. Some will need water every day, but some won't. It depends on the pot, the soil, position, etc (see *Watering* on page 8). So always check how damp the soil is by inserting your finger 3 cm or so into it. Do not water the plant unless the soil is dry or becoming dry.
◆ In summer most houseplants need feeding at least fortnightly. Follow the instructions that come with the fertiliser you have chosen, remembering that over-feeding does not produce bigger and better plants, usually it sets them back, and sometimes kills them.
◆ Mist your plants regularly with and hand-held atomiser, especially in very hot, dry weather. You may find your plants appreciate being grouped together in summer to increase local humidity.
◆ Move your plants around so that they all get a share of the good light areas, and be careful not to place plants too close to windows in the middle of the day.
◆ Be particularly vigilant in regard to checking for pests and diseases. Summer is when they are most active.

WHAT TO DO IN AUTUMN

This is the time to gradually reduce the water and fertiliser you give your plants. But once again, let your plants tell you how much water they need.

◆ Check the soil daily by inserting your finger 3 cm into it. It it is moist, do not water.
◆ By the last month of autumn you should have stopped feeding your plants with the exception of those plants that flower in the autumn such as *Cyclamen*.
◆ If you start heating the house in autumn, make sure you move plants away from heaters and out of draughts.

WHAT TO DO IN WINTER

Even plants growing in the most perfect situation can droop in winter when rooms are artificially heated. Here are some survival techniques.

◆ Buy your plants in spring and throw them out at the end of autumn. This is a fairly drastic, and rather expensive option, but it is better to have no houseplants in winter than a collection of dead or dying ones.
◆ Take them outside in winter. This only works if you live in a frost-free area and if you have a spot that's sheltered from cold winds (the north side of a house is ideal). Not all of your plants will survive this treatment, but those that do will undoubtedly benefit. Plants would much rather be cold all the time than alternately hot and cold, as they are with the artificial heating of a house. The other reason they benefit by wintering out of doors is that most plants are native to tropical or subtropical areas and need some humidity. The air inside a heated house is extremely dry - as dry as a desert.
◆ Group your plants together in winter in the sunniest room. This grouping of plants produces local humidity. You could try putting them, still in their pots, in a large tray on a layer of pebbles. Pour water over the pebbles, but don't cover them with water. The pots should not be standing in water. The idea is to produce a vapour bath. Check the water level periodically. In heated rooms a dish of water placed near your plants is another way to produce humidity.

In frost-free areas, put houseplants outside on wet days. Rainwater makes a huge difference to their health.

Dangerous Plants

It is wise to keep these plants out of the reach of children.

◆ *Dieffenbachia.* The sap in this plant contains a poison which swells the glands in the throat.
◆ Prickly cactuses such as *Schlumbergera*, *Rebutia*, *Chamaecereus sylvestri* and *Mammillaria bosasana* can prick inquisitive fingers.

A to Z of Indoor Plants

Above ◆ **ACHIMENES LONGIFLORA**
Right ◆ **ADIANTUM HISPIDULUM**

Achimenes

HOT WATER PLANT

Achimenes varieties are attractive, bushy little plants which require special conditions to thrive. They range in height from about 10-70 cm, the longer stemmed varieties often trailing, which makes them suitable for hanging baskets. *Achimenes* die back in autumn leaving only the thick root-like underground tubers from which the plants will grow again in spring. The dark green foliage is covered with fine hairs and the flowers are in shades of red, pink, violet, white and orange, sometimes spotted and with white throats. Each bloom lasts for only a few days but the plant flowers for a long period from summer into autumn. As days shorten and the temperature drops, flowering stops, leaves wither and the plant becomes dormant until spring.

LIGHT While growing, *Achimenes* species need bright light but not direct sunlight.

TEMPERATURE A slightly warm room with a temperature of 18°-20°C is best. Plants will tolerate up to 5°C cooler but will soon collapse if the temperature rises higher than 26°C. During winter the dormant plant is unaffected by cool temperatures, but should be kept out of frosty areas.

WATERING AND FEEDING Good drainage is essential, but the plant should be well watered once growth has started. Be sure water is not accumulating in the saucer. Following the maker's directions use a high nitrogen liquid fertiliser until flower buds appear then change to a fertiliser with a higher percentage of phosphate and potassium.

SPECIAL CARE When temperature rises increase the humidity and use fine mist spray around plant. After flowering stops the stems will die and should be cut back to soil level. Repot in spring as soon as new shoots appear. Pinch back to encourage bushy growth.

COMMON PROBLEMS If flower buds discolour and drop they have probably been affected by heat. Lack of flowers may be caused by lack of light.

Adiantum

MAIDENHAIR FERN

These ferns are among the most decorative indoor plants and are suitable for pots or hanging baskets. There are several varieties, whose foliage ranges from very fine to coarse, stems from pale brown to black and height from 20-40 cm. The fronds spring from thickened root-like stems spreading horizontally just below the surface of the soil. New growth occurs throughout the year but is most abundant in spring. Sporecases, the fern's equivalent to flower seeds, develop on the underside of some of the older fronds, making the foliage turn brown.

LIGHT Bright but no direct sunlight.
TEMPERATURE Normal room temperature ranging from 10°-24°C. Certain species from tropical areas are susceptible to cold weather.
WATERING AND FEEDING Drying out of the root ball can be fatal, although the soil should be moist rather than waterlogged. Less water will be needed in winter. Fertilise monthly using half strength liquid fertiliser high in nitrogen or follow manufacturer's instructions.
SPECIAL CARE Keep the humidity high, particularly in hot weather —double potting is especially good for maidenhairs. Plants need fresh air but must be kept out of draughts. Most will not thrive in air polluted by cooking fumes. Repot in spring only if roots have been forced to the surface of the original pot.
COMMON PROBLEMS It is natural for old fronds to dry out and die, and for brown clusters of spore cases to appear on the undersides of leaflets. However, browning of all fronds is probably

Aechmea

URN PLANT/VASE PLANT

These are tropical plants, belonging to the Bromeliad family. They are mainly tree dwellers whose leaves are arranged in a vase shape to catch and hold rain. The flower stalk rises from the centre of a rosette of leaves and carries many small flowers which are supported by coloured bracts. The brightly coloured flower head lasts for a long time but when it dies, the leaf rosette dies with it, leaving several small offsets around the base. It will take at least three years for a young *Aechmea* to reach flowering stage. Of the varieties available the hybrid 'Foster's Favourite' (A. x 'Foster's Favourite'), with its dark red leaves, purple flowers and deep red berries, is one of the easiest to grow indoors.

LIGHT Direct sunlight or very bright light. Variegated leaf forms need plenty of light to hold their leaf patterns.
TEMPERATURE Not less than 16°C for good growth.
WATERING AND FEEDING Keep the centre of the rosette filled with fresh water, the soil barely moist. Feed only from spring to autumn, every 2-3 weeks. Very dilute fish emulsions are good.
SPECIAL CARE *Aechmea* species, particularly those with thin leaves, like high humidity. Annual repotting is not necessary.
COMMON PROBLEMS If temperature is too cool foliage may turn yellow. Watch for scale on leaves and thrips on flowers.

Left ◆ AECHMEA X MAGINALII

Above ◆ **AEONIUM**
Below ◆ **AESCHYNANTHUS X 'BLACK PAGODA'**

SPECIAL CARE *Aeonium* species prefer a dry atmosphere and a well-drained soil. Repot large plants annually and small ones every few years at the start of the growing season using terracotta pots if possible.

COMMON PROBLEMS Usually trouble free. Too little water causes wrinkled leaves; too much produces flabby ones.

Aeschynanthus

LIPSTICK PLANT/BASKET PLANT

There are four or five different varieties of this plant usually available and all make attractive hanging plants, provided they can be given the right conditions. The flowers appear in summer in shades of red, orange or yellow: either clustered at the end of the stems as in the basket plant, *Aeschynanthus speciosus*, or scattered along them as in the lipstick plant, *A. lobbianus*. The hybrid 'Black Pagoda' bears flowers all year round and, like its parent, *A. marmoratus*, is grown also for its attractive foliage, variegated on both surfaces.

LIGHT Bright light especially for those with variegated leaves but little direct sunlight.

TEMPERATURE Normal room temperature of 18°-20°C. A resting period with lower temperature in winter will encourage bud formation.

WATERING AND FEEDING Hanging baskets tend to dry out easily so water frequently, particularly when the plant is in flower. Reduce water as weather cools to encourage a resting period. Use a liquid or slow-release fertiliser as directed by maker.

SPECIAL CARE After flowering, cut backs stems to encourage new shoots. Humid atmosphere is essential for good growth. Repot only when container is full of roots.

COMMON PROBLEMS Aphids may be a pest. Draughts and lack of water can cause leaves to fall off.

Aeonium

These succulent plants have distinctive rosettes of fleshy leaves at the tip of stems formed as the lower leaves of the rosette die. In some species such as *Aeonium canariense*, the stems are very short; in others they branch, making small leggy shrubs up to 90 cm in height. The sprays of small flowers, mostly cream coloured, grow from the centre of each rosette when the plant is several years old. Having flowered once, that particular rosette dies.

LIGHT Full sunlight.

TEMPERATURE Warm room, around 20°C. A lower temperature in winter will induce beneficial dormancy.

WATERING AND FEEDING Allow the top 1 cm or so of soil to dry out between waterings during the growing season. When dormant reduce watering further. Use liquid or slow-release fertiliser as directed by manufacturer.

Aglaonema

CHINESE EVERGREEN/PAINTED DROP-TONGUE/CHINESE LUCKY PLANT

These popular evergreen plants are grown for their attractive variegated foliage patterned in grey, cream and green. Long-stemmed leaves grow from the centres of several shoots and well-established plants may eventually reach 90 cm in height. The tiny flowers cover a central spike surrounded by a white or yellow spathe, rather like a very small monstera flower head. The waxy, plain green Chinese evergreen, *Aglaonema modestum*, is particularly hardy. It tolerates lower temperatures than more showy types, and an old plant may be cut back to ground level in late winter to rejuvenate it. Painted drop-tongue, *A. roebelinii* 'Silver Queen', with its dark green and silver variegated leaves is another popular variety.

LIGHT Aglaonemas will thrive in medium light, even in artificially lit hallways where other plants fail. Direct sunlight will burn he leaves.

TEMPERATURE Normal room temperature or slightly warmer but not less than 10°C for most varieties.

WATERING AND FEEDING While plants are growing actively, keep the soil moist but not sodden and apply liquid or slow-release fertiliser. In winter reduce water supply and do not use fertiliser.

SPECIAL CARE *Aglaonema* species like a humid atmosphere and should be mist-sprayed during spells of hot, dry weather. Repot only after two or three years as these plants prefer to be slightly pot-bound.

COMMON PROBLEMS
Old plants normally shed the lower leaves but yellowing and excessive leaf drop may be caused by too much light. If margins of leaves turn brown, increase the humidity. Watch for spider mites, aphids and mealy bugs especially at higher temperatures.

Above ◆ **AGLAONEMA COMMUTATUM**

Above ◆ **ALOCASIA CUPREA**

Alocasia

ELEPHANT'S EARS/ CUNJEVOI/SPOON LILY

Large foliage plants from the tropics, *Alocasia* species can be grown successfully indoors if enough warmth and humidity are provided. Even indoors they can become large plants with arrow-shaped leaves up to 60 cm in length and 30 cm in width and therefore they need plenty of space to grow. Foliage is usually green but sometimes bronze and the underside dull purple or patterned by a pale network of veins. The flower heads are insignificant, rather like small arum lilies. The cunjevoi or spoon lily, *A. macrorrhizos*, is the most easily grown but is poisonous if eaten.

LIGHT Medium to bright filtered light but no direct sunlight.

TEMPERATURE Plenty of warmth day and night, up to 27°C while actively growing and not less than 13°C when dormant in winter.

WATERING AND FEEDING Keep the soil thoroughly moist during the growing season, and allow the top 3-4 cm to dry out between waterings in cold weather. Use high-nitrogen liquid fertiliser or a slow-release variety when growth starts until the onset of cooler weather.

SPECIAL CARE High humidity is important; spraying and wiping the leaves with a damp cloth will help in a dry atmosphere. Repot in summer only when the roots fill the pot.

COMMON PROBLEMS
Poor growth usually indicates insufficient warmth and humidity. Leaves die as they get old. Watch for mealy bugs.

Aloe

PARTRIDGE-BREASTED ALOE

There are hundreds of varieties of these adaptable succulents, many of them suitable for growing indoors. Most have fleshy, spiny-edged, elongated triangular leaves, some forming tightly packed rosettes, others carried on long stems. The tubular flowers are borne on open spikes which appear between the leaves from late winter to summer. One of the most popular and easily grown is the partridge-breasted aloe, *Aloe variegata*, which forms a small rosette of dark grey-green spineless leaves unevenly marked in white transverse bands. The flowers are flesh pink on stems 30 cm in height.

LIGHT Bright light for all varieties and direct sunlight for those with spiny leaves.

TEMPERATURE Aloes grow well at normal room temperature. To encourage flowering they should be given a short winter rest at a temperature of 10°C or below.

WATERING AND FEEDING Keep soil thoroughly moist when plants are growing but greatly restrict water when they are dormant, while not allowing the soil to dry out completely. Fertilise only during growing period.

SPECIAL CARE *Aloe* species prefer a dry atmosphere. Water should not be allowed to stand in the rosettes. Repot annually in spring into a pot one size larger.

COMMON PROBLEMS Decay at the base of the leaves may be caused by leaving water standing in rosettes. Mealy bugs attack both leaves and roots, hiding deep in the rosette or under the soil.

Above ◆ **ALOE VERA**

Below ◆ **ANANAS COMOSUS VARIEGATUS**

Ananas Comosus 'Variegatus'

VARIEGATED PINEAPPLE PLANT/STRIPED WILD PINEAPPLE

This small, slow-growing bromeliad is a variegated variety of the edible pineapple. The striped grey-green leaves have sharply-toothed creamy margins which change to pink when grown in sunlight. After five or six years a flower spike rises from the centre of the rosette of leaves. It may reach 90 cm in height and may develop a miniature pineapple topped with a tuft of leaves. Other varieties include the much larger striped wild pineapple, *Ananas bracteatus* 'Striatus' which also has large, cream, green and pink striped leaves but rarely flowers indoors and the dwarf, dark green *A. nanus* which produces hard, dark green fruit.

LIGHT Bright light, including direct sunlight.

TEMPERATURE A warm room all the year round.

WATERING AND FEEDING Keep the soil moist but allow the top to dry out before rewatering. Use liquid or slow-release fertiliser as directed by the manufacturer.

SPECIAL CARE High humidity is required. Use a spray in hot, dry weather. Repot in spring.

COMMON PROBLEMS Like other bromeliads, once the flower has developed a fruit the plant dies. A new plant may be grown by cutting the cluster of leaves and a slice of the flesh from the top of the fruit. Allow the cutting to dry for a few days before potting into a sandy mix.

Anthurium

FLAMINGO FLOWER/PAINTER'S PALETTE/CRYSTAL ANTHURIUM/OILCLOTH FLOWER/PIGTAIL PLANT/STRAP FLOWER

These tropical plants can be divided into two groups, those grown for their striking looks and long-lasting blooms such as the painter's palette and flamingo flower, *Anthurium andreanum* and *A. scherzerianum*, and those grown for their showy foliage such as *A. crystallinum*. The flower heads have long slender stalks topped by a palette or shield-shaped spathe and a narrow spike (spadix), 6-7 cm in length, of tiny, closely packed flowers. In the flamingo flower, *A. scherzerianum*, the spathe is about 10 cm long, glossy scarlet, occasionally speckled in white, and the curled and twisted spadix is orange. In the many hybrids of *A. andreanum* the highly polished spathe may be red, orange, pink or white and the arching spadix a pale yellow.

Above ◆ **ANTHURIUM CRYSTALLINUM**

Foliage species of *Anthurium* are much more difficult to grow as they need constant high humidity not usually found in houses. As they mature the long-stalked, heart-shaped, velvety leaves of *A. crystallinum* change from purplish bronze to deep green, patterned in silvery white by the network of veins. The flowers of these types of *Anthurium* are insignificant.

LIGHT Good filtered light, not necessarily bright and no direct sunlight.

TEMPERATURE These plants thrive at 20°C but tolerate much lower levels for short periods.

WATERING AND FEEDING Keep the soil well watered during the growing period but allow the top 2 cm to dry out between waterings when the plants are resting. Fertilise every second week with a liquid feed while in active growth or use slow-release pills or sticks.

SPECIAL CARE Flowering plants are quite happy in a normal room but will flower more freely in a humid atmosphere. Repot annually in spring. A. crystallinum needs very high humidity.

COMMON PROBLEMS Yellowing of foliage is often the result of excessive light, but yellow speckling may be caused by red spider.

Aphelandra Squarrosa

ZEBRA PLANT/SAFFRON SPIKE

The zebra plant takes its main common name from its large dark green leaves heavily striped in white and the other, saffron spike, from the flower heads of long-lasting orange-yellow bracts and small yellow flowers. Plants may reach 30 cm in height and blooms appear in spring. It is best to buy a plant already in flower as it is difficult to initiate flowering. There are several different varieties of *Aphelandra squarrosa* but all are similar in appearance and size. The

Above ◆ **APHELANDRA SQUARROSA**
Right ◆ **APOROCACTUS FLAGELLIFORMIS**

container may appear to be too small for the plants but zebra plants prefer a slightly pot-bound existence.

LIGHT Bright light but not direct sunlight.

TEMPERATURE A warm room is best during the growing season (about 20°C), but a cooler position while resting in winter.

WATERING AND FEEDING Keep well watered but not sodden while growing and reduce watering to allow the top 3-4 cm to dry out in winter. Fertilise regularly during active growth. Too much nitrogen will encourage leaf rather than flower growth.

SPECIAL CARE Zebra plants need plenty of humidity to thrive especially when flowering. When the plant is not actively growing, a drier atmosphere is tolerated.

COMMON PROBLEMS Leaf-drop can be caused by too low a temperature or a sudden change in temperature. Browning of leaf margins and brown leaf spots can be caused by lack of humidity.

Aporocactus Flagelliformis

RAT'S TAIL CACTUS

Despite its name, this easily grown cactus makes an attractive hanging basket as the long, trailing stems produce an abundance of cerise flowers for several weeks in spring. Stems may reach more than 1 m in length and as they are covered in cactus spines the basket should be kept well away from any passageway. If grown in a pot the stems should be encouraged to grow evenly around the pot or it may overbalance.

LIGHT Direct sunlight. If possible put the container out of doors for a few weeks after flowering.

TEMPERATURE Normal room temperature while flowering, cooler conditions for the resting period in winter.

WATERING AND FEEDING Keep the soil thoroughly moist in the growing period but allow it to become almost dry during winter. Feed during the growing period by spraying half-strength liquid fertiliser on the stems every other week.

SPECIAL CARE These are easily grown plants needing no special conditions. Repot annually in rich potting mix after flowering.

COMMON PROBLEMS None.

Araucaria Heterophylla
(SYN. A. EXCELSA)

NORFOLK ISLAND PINE/CHRISTMAS TREE PLANT/AUSTRALIAN PINE OR HOUSE PINE/HOOP PINE

Although this well-known tree grows to a height of 60 m when planted in a garden, it will take many years to reach 2 m if confined in a pot. Its symmetrical shape and horizontal branches make it ideal as a Christmas tree although the pliable branches of young specimens will support only the lightest decorations. The young spring foliage is soft, bright green which gradually darkens as it matures.

LIGHT Medium to bright but no direct sunlight.

TEMPERATURE Normal room temperature but a wide range, 5°-25°C, is tolerated.

WATERING AND FEEDING Keep the soil well watered but not sodden while the tree is growing. Allow the top 2-3 cm of soil to dry between waterings in cool weather. Feed with standard fertiliser through spring and summer.

SPECIAL CARE Mist spray on hot days. Be sure ventilation is good, but do not allow the plant to stand in a draught. Repot in spring about every third year when roots fill the container.

COMMON PROBLEMS Excessive needle-fall may be caused by lack of light and lower branches may drop if soil is too dry or in a dormant period, too wet. Watch for mealy bugs.

Archontophoenix

ALEXANDRA PALM/BANGALOW PALM/STEP PALM

Although not as hardy indoors as the popular Kentia palms these two Australian natives, the Alexandra palm, *Archontophoenix alexandrae*, and the Bangalow palm, *A. cunninghamiana*, are useful while young as tall plants to bring interest to big brightly lit spaces. Both have smooth trunks with feathery leaves arching out from the crown. The underside of the Alexandra palm's foliage is covered with fine silvery hairs and the Bangalow's is hairless and green. The Bangalow grows faster, reaching 4-5 m in ten years in good conditions.

LIGHT Good, bright light but not direct sunlight.

TEMPERATURE Normal warm room temperature. The Bangalow tolerates cooler conditions than the Alexandra palm.

WATERING AND FEEDING Keep well-drained soil moist at all times. Use slow-release fertilisers.

SPECIAL CARE Damage to the terminal bud will prevent the production of new fronds and may cause the plant to die. Cuts on the trunk will cause spreading decay. Both palms are native to swampy areas and need humid atmosphere. Repot when growing actively if roots fill the pot.

COMMON PROBLEMS Watch for scale, red spider and mealy bugs; the latter may occur above and below ground. Poor growth is usually the result of a lack of light and humidity.

Above ◆ ARCHONTOPHOENIX ALEXANDRAE
Left ◆ ARAUCARIA HETEROPHYLLA

Ardisia Crenata
(SYN. A. CRENULATA)
CORAL BERRY/SPICE BERRY

Known as coral berry for its bright red fruit, this attractive indoor plant is deservedly popular. The glossy dark green leaves contrast with the pale pinky-white flowers of early summer followed by the bright red berries which are held until the next flowering season. Often a plant has only a single stem which may reach 90 cm in height although in a mature plant, a cluster of two or three stems is more attractive.

LIGHT Bright with direct morning sunlight.

TEMPERATURE Cool, but not below 7°C. If the temperature rises, increase humidity.

WATERING AND FEEDING Soil should be kept moist during the growing season but the top 1-2 cm allowed to dry out in winter. Feed with liquid fertiliser every second week in spring and summer or use slow-release fertiliser.

SPECIAL CARE Mist spray during summer on hot dry days. Cut off stems of spent berries. Repot mature plants each spring into the same pot, replacing some of

the potting mix with a fresh supply. Young plants will require a pot one size larger.

COMMON PROBLEMS If berries fall too soon after ripening, the humidity may be too low.

Arecastrum Romanzoffium
QUEEN PALM

The queen palm is a tall feather-leafed palm sometimes called by its old botanical name of *Cocos plumosa*. It is often grown outdoors but is a suitable indoor plant in its young stages and, as it grows, for high-ceilinged rooms. The trunk is smooth and grey and the long, arching fronds make it one of the most graceful of the palms. When young the queen palm has undivided leaves about 1 m in length and 10 cm wide but these are gradually replaced by upright

feather-like leaves which are in turn superseded by long, weeping adult fronds.

LIGHT Bright with some direct sunlight.

TEMPERATURE This palm will tolerate a wide range of temperature.

WATERING AND FEEDING Keep the soil moist but do not stand in water. Use slow-release fertilisers.

SPECIAL CARE Prefers a humid atmosphere. Keep leaves dust free by wiping with a damp cloth. Repot when roots fill the container.

COMMON PROBLEMS Watch for mealy bugs particularly at the base of fronds and in the soil.

Below Left ◆ **ARECASTRUM ROMANZOFFIUM**
Below ◆ **ASPARAGUS DENSIFLORUS 'SPRENGERI'**
Right ◆ **ARDISIA**

Asparagus

ASPARAGUS FERN/SPRENGER'S ASPARAGUS/EMERALD FEATHER/FOXTAIL ASPARAGUS

In spite of their common name asparagus fern, these plants are not true ferns but belong to the lily family. Most have fine foliage which gives them a fern-like appearance. There are a number of different species widely available, most of them grown for their attractive foliage. Only one, Sprenger's asparagus or emerald feather, *Asparagus densiflorus* 'Sprengeri', commonly bears white flowers which are later followed by bright red berries. It is one of the hardiest of the asparagus ferns and will even survive a certain degree of neglect. Another well-known type is often seen climbing rampantly in the garden; this is the asparagus fern, *A. setaceus* (formerly *A. plumosus*). It has the finest, most fern-like foliage of the popular species and is best known as an indoor plant in its dwarf variety *A. setaceus* 'Nanus'. These plants do not climb when young and even when mature their stems will not be much more than 1.5 m in length. The foxtail asparagus, *A. densiflorus* 'Myers', is another popular variety, in which the trailing plant stems (up to 90 cm in length) are surrounded by fine, pale green needle-like foliage. The species known as smilax, *A. asparagoides*, which has long narrow leaves, is occasionally found today but was particularly popular in the last century when it was known by its botanical name, *A. medeoloides*. It is a vigorous climber, twining itself around any support it can reach. While Sprenger's asparagus with its trailing branches is used in hanging baskets, asparagus ferns may be trained around an entire basket to create a feathery green globe.

LIGHT Bright but no direct sunlight. Sprenger's asparagus will tolerate less light than the others.

Above ◆ **ASPARAGUS MYERSII**
Below ◆ **ASPIDISTRA ELATIOR**

TEMPERATURE A moderately warm room, not below 10°C in winter.

WATERING AND FEEDING Water well when growing but in winter water only enough to prevent the soil from drying out. Use a high nitrogen fertiliser following maker's instructions.

SPECIAL CARE To encourage the plants to be bushy, pinch back tips (not of the foxtail fern, which grows very slowly). Repot in spring if necessary, although asparagus ferns do not mind being slightly pot bound.

COMMON PROBLEMS Leaf-fall may be caused by insufficient light or lack of moisture in the soil especially if temperatures are high.

Aspidistra Elatior

ASPIDISTRA/CAST IRON PLANT

A tough evergreen perennial, the aspidistra has long been used for indoor decoration because of its ability to withstand cold, neglect, poor light and polluted air. However its long, dark green leaves, which spring from a thickened root system, respond to good treatment making a handsome, rich green plant up to 50 cm tall. Dark, bell-shaped flowers are borne at soil level but are rarely noticed because they are screened by the leaves. A variegated variety, *A. elatior* 'Variegata', with cream and green striped leaves is particularly attractive.

LIGHT Tolerates poorly lit areas but thrives in a medium light. The striped variety needs better light. Direct sunlight will burn the leaves.

TEMPERATURE Normal room temperature.

WATERING AND FEEDING Keep soil just moist for best results and make sure the pot does not stand in water. During growing season use standard fertilisers following maker's instructions.

SPECIAL CARE Wipe the leaves free of dust with a damp cloth. Repot in early spring if roots have filled container. A soft plastic container may not be strong enough. If transplanting a clump from the garden, look out for snails.

COMMON PROBLEMS Strong sunlight may burn the leaves. Watch for scale.

Asplenium

BIRD'S NEST FERN/MOTHER SPLEENWORT/HEN-AND CHICKEN FERN/PARSLEY FERN

The two most commonly grown forms of this group of ferns are so different in appearance it is hard to believe that they are closely related. Each grows from a single crown, the fronds spraying out all around it. The bird's nest fern, *Asplenium australasicum* (or *A. nidus*, a very similar Asian species), has long, narrow, undivided fronds with a brown or black central rib. They are arranged in a rosette which, in their native rainforests, collects rain and falling organic matter needed for growth. A mature bird's nest fern may measure 1.5-2 m across but because of its small root system it is suitable for growing in a container. The mother spleenwort, *A. bulbiferum*, also has large, metre-long fronds but these are triangular in outline and much divided creating a feathery appearance. Baby plantlets appear on many of the tips of mature fronds and by the time the frond dies, the plantlets should be large enough to be potted in small containers. When young, mother spleenworts are excellent for containers but must eventually be put in the garden when they become too large.

LIGHT Medium light and no direct sunlight.

TEMPERATURE Normal room temperature but not below 13°C in winter.

WATERING AND FEEDING Keep the soil moist but not waterlogged. During spring and summer use half-strength liquid fertiliser.

SPECIAL CARE Wipe the fronds of the bird's nest fern regularly with a damp cloth once they are mature enough to handle. Keep the atmosphere humid. Young foliage may be burnt by full strength insecticides so test-spray a small area first. Repot in spring if the pot is root-bound: immerse the newly planted pot in water for half an hour, then lift drain.

Top ◆ **ASPLENIUM NIDUS**

Left ◆ **ASPLENIUM BULBIFERUM**

COMMON PROBLEMS Browning of foliage is often caused by lack of moisture in the soil or dry atmosphere. Velvety brown bands on the underside of the foliage are normal sporecases. Wedge-shaped brown or black areas in the foliage may be caused by nematodes. Watch for scale and mealy bug.

Athyrium Australe

AUSTRAL LADY FERN

This is a native fern which grows quickly and easily if given a little attention. Long, arching, soft green fronds grow up to 2 m in length and are deeply divided. A short trunk is sometimes formed giving the plant the appearance of a small tree-fern. Unlike the somewhat similar mother spleenwort, the Austral lady fern does

Above ♦ **AUCUBA JAPONICA 'VARIEGATA'**
Below ♦ **ATHYRIUM AUSTRALE**

not bear young plantlets but mature fronds may have lines of pale brown sporecases on their undersides.

LIGHT Medium to filtered bright light but no direct sunlight.

TEMPERATURE Normal room temperature.

WATERING AND FEEDING Keep the soil moist but not waterlogged and feed with slow-release or half-strength liquid fertiliser.

SPECIAL CARE A humid atmosphere is preferable but the plant will tolerate drier spells. Avoid draughts. Repotting annually in very early spring will probably be necessary.

COMMON PROBLEMS Watch for scale, aphids and mealy bugs.

Aucuba Japonica 'Variegata'

SPOTTED LAUREL/GOLD DUST PLANT/JAPANESE LAUREL

These evergreen shrubs are popular plants for shady places in the garden but they also make good indoor plants for unheated rooms. Outside they may grow to 3-4 m in height but when the root system is restricted in a container they seldom reach more than 1 m. The glossy green leaves of *Aucuba japonica* 'Variegata' are thickly dusted with gold but there are other varieties with different variegations. The flowers are insignificant and scarlet berries will be produced only when male and female plants are grown close together.

LIGHT Bright, filtered sunlight.

TEMPERATURE Prefers cool rooms and will not thrive in temperatures over 23°C.

WATERING AND FEEDING Keep the soil moist throughout the year, and feed liquid or slow-release fertiliser as the maker directs.

SPECIAL CARE Needs humidity if the temperature rises, but is one of few plants unaffected by draughts. Prune lightly in late winter to encourage bushy growth. Repot at the same time if necessary, although these plants do not need large pots. Keep leaves dust free with a damp cloth.

COMMON PROBLEMS Watch for scale.

Beaucarnea Recurvata

PONY TAIL

This slow-growing succulent from Mexico's arid areas is one of the easiest indoor plants to care for. Although in the open it may reach 6 m in height, its size is greatly restricted in a container. When young it looks like a large onion, as the short stem is swollen with stored water and the long thin curving leaves spray out from the top. The stem lengthens as it ages but the base remains swollen. The pony tail is unlikely to flower indoors.

LIGHT Bright with some direct sunlight.

TEMPERATURE The pony tail tolerates a wide range of temperatures.

WATERING AND FEEDING
When the plant is actively growing, water only enough to moisten the soil. Allow the top few centimetres to dry out before watering again. During the rest period in winter water only sufficiently to stop the soil drying out altogether. Add a little slow-release fertiliser at the start of the growing season.

SPECIAL CARE Keep the leaves free of spider's webs and dust. Repot only if the roots have filled the container as the pony tail prefers a slightly pot-bound condition. Use a heavy pot to balance the weight of the plant.

COMMON PROBLEMS
Slower growth than normal may be the result of too little light.

Begonia

BEGONIA

Begonias form a very large and varied group of plants, many of which make ideal indoor plants because of their tolerance of shady places. They may be divided into three main groups according to their root systems; some have a fibrous root system composed of

Above ◆ **BEGONIA TUBERHYBRIDS**
Left ◆ **BEAUCARNEA RECURVATA**
Right ◆ **BEGONIAS IN BLOOM**

many small roots similar to most garden shrubs, while others have a thickened underground stem, a rhizome, from which both roots and leaves grow. These two groups require similar conditions, and are therefore described together. The third main group, characterised by having tubers which are underground storage organs, is described separately.

The flowers of begonias may be in large clusters of small flowers or small groups of large showy flowers. The male flowers are the most spectacular but last for only a few days, while the small female flowers, which are distinguished by a prominent coloured, three-angled ovary behind the petals, may last for several weeks. The flowers of some begonias are perfumed.

The fibrous rooted begonias are grown for both their foliage and their flowers. Among the taller plants in this group are tree begonias which range from 1.5-2.5 m in height and have leaves shaped like angel's wings. In some, such as the variety, 'Mrs Christian Thornett', the leaves are green spotted with white, while others have dull red or bronze undersides to their foliage. The flowers form in drooping bunches in summer and autumn, and are mainly white, pink, red or soft orange.

Tuberous Begonia

Tuberous begonias have the capacity to store food in their tubers and therefore generally die back during the winter months and shoot afresh in spring. However, some maintain their foliage in the cold weather although not actively growing. Begonias of this group are among the most difficult to grow especially those with enormous flowers which may be up to 30 cm across and are usually frilled and ruffled. These are more easily grown in glass houses, but those of the Grandiflora Compacta group, whose blossoms, 8-10 cm in diameter, are carried on strong stems extending well clear of the foliage, are more amenable to normal room conditions. Tuberous begonia flowers, either single or double, are white, pink, red, yellow or cream. Most are summer flowerers but a hybrid group, which are not true tuberous begonias, bloom in the winter and are usually discarded after flowering.

LIGHT Bright filtered light during the growing season.

TEMPERATURE Normal room temperature (below 20°C) during active growth. Both leafless and leafy tubers should be kept in a cool position in the winter.

WATERING AND FEEDING Keep the soil moist but allow the top to dry out between waterings. As cool weather arrives and foliage yellows, decrease the amount of water until only enough is given to stop the soil from drying out. Feed while growing, preferably a complete fertiliser with a high potash (K) content.

SPECIAL CARE Increase the humidity in hot, dry weather. To increase the size of the male flower, the small female flowers, which flank the male on each side, may be carefully removed when they first appear. Repot in early spring, keeping the tuber hollowside up.

COMMON PROBLEMS Watch for powdery mildew. It is normal for the leaves to yellow and fall when flowering finishes.

The smaller fibrous rooted begonias make rounded bushes and are often used to decorate the edges of flower beds. The foliage may be green or soft bronze and the single or double flowers white, pink or red. This group includes the well-known 'Thousand Wonders' and the bronze-leafed 'Pink Camellia' with small double pink flowers. Begonias with swollen root-like underground rhizomes are grown mainly for their foliage. The flowers are generally small, pink and insignificant but the leaves are often large and patterned in a variety of colours including silver and shades of plum, purple, bronze green and red. Many are hybrids often referred to as rex begonias, the descendants of *B. rex*. They are usually rounded or sprawling plants, 20-40 cm in height with individual leaves up to 25-30 cm long. Both fibrous rooted and rhizomatous begonias require similar conditions.

LIGHT Those grown for foliage need diffused sunlight but those grown for flowers will need some direct sun, but not hot midday rays, to produce plenty of blooms.

TEMPERATURE Normal room temperature while growing but a cooler atmosphere, not below 13°C in the resting period.

WATERING AND FEEDING Avoid overwatering, keep the soil moist but not soggy. If accidentally dried out, submerge the pot in a bucket of water for about 20 minutes, then allow to drain. Restrict water in the resting period. Fertilise only in the growing season.

SPECIAL CARE Keep the atmosphere humid. Plants prefer a warm, humid, draught-free position. When repotting in early spring, cut out the oldest canes in tree begonias if necessary. Pinch back young shoots in dwarf types to encourage bushiness. Keep rhizomes on the surface when repotting.

COMMON PROBLEMS Powdery mildew causes the leaves to darken and shrivel; nematodes also will cause the leaves to shrivel at the base.

Billbergia Nutans

QUEEN'S TEARS/FRIENDSHIP PLANT

This member of the bromeliad group is one of the easiest plants to grow both indoors and out. The long, thin, stiff leaves, edged with small teeth, arch out and form narrow rosettes packed tightly against each other. The elongated tubular flowers, patterned in green, pink and blue, hang in colourful clusters from stems covered in bright pink bracts. The plant multiplies quickly and soon fills the pot. Flowers usually appear in spring but may come intermittently throughout the year.

LIGHT Bright, with several hours of direct sunlight.

TEMPERATURE Normal room temperature but will survive cooler conditions, even frosty weather for a few days if left outside.

Below ◆ **BILLBERGIA NUTANS**
Right ◆ **BLECHNUM GIBBUM**

WATERING AND FEEDING

As for other bromeliads, keep the rosettes filled with fresh water and the soil just moist. Use liquid or slow-release fertiliser following the maker's directions.

SPECIAL CARE Remove dead flowers. Repot in spring if roots fill the pot.

COMMON PROBLEMS The weight of the foliage may cause the plant to overbalance. Use a ceramic or terracotta pot to counteract this.

Blechnum

WATER FERN/BRAZIL TREE FERN/ HAMMOCK FERN

Water ferns are so called because of their preference for damp, even swampy conditions. Those most commonly grown have long, narrow, arching fronds divided almost to the centre rib.

Mature fronds, which vary from 0.25-1.5 m in length according to

species, may be pale green and soft or dark green and leathery.

In some the young foliage is pink-tipped. In mature plants the spore-producing fronds are very often different in shape from the others.

LIGHT Bright but filtered, no direct sunlight.

TEMPERATURE Most water ferns such as *Blechnum gibbum* from New Caledonia, are native to warmer climates and prefer a warm room. However some Australian species such as the Lance water fern, *B. chambersii* from Victoria, are happy in lower temperatures.

WATERING AND FEEDING Keep the soil well-watered while the fern is actively growing but water infrequently during winter. Feed sparingly during the growing season with half-strength liquid fertiliser or follow the maker's directions for ferns.

SPECIAL CARE A humid atmosphere especially when growth is most active. Keep out of draughts. Repot only when plant roots fill the pot.

COMMON PROBLEMS Brown growths on the underside of the fronds are normal reproductive sporecases. Lack of new leaves may be caused by fertiliser burning the new fronds. Brown bands on the foliage are caused by nematodes, but overall browning may be the result of a dry atmosphere and lack of water.

Bulbs, Flowering

Potted bulbs and other flowering bulbous plants are available in nurseries at certain times of the year. Bulb species include daffodils, tulips, lily-of-the-valley, autumn crocus, *Lachenalia*, *Hippeastrum* and *Vallota* (Scarborough lilies). Hyacinths are dealt with in a separate entry. Most flowering bulbs are not permanent indoor plants and should only be kept inside while the flowers last. They

should then be discarded or planted out in the garden where they may produce flowers the following year. Some, such as *Lachenalia*, *Hippeastrum* and Scarborough lilies, will flower again the following year if kept in pots.

LIGHT Bulbs prefer a well-lit position close to a window, but little if any direct sunlight. No direct sun for lily-of-the-valley.

TEMPERATURE Normal room temperature with good ventilation. Cooler conditions will result in longer lasting flowers.

WATERING AND FEEDING Keep moist but not wet until planting out in the garden when the flowers fade or when the leaves die down. After this, gradually cease watering. Feed only those that are to remain in pots, using a complete liquid or slow-release fertiliser high in potash.

SPECIAL CARE When buying, look for plants with flowers just coming into bloom. The flowers of small daffodils such as

hoop petticoats are less likely to topple over than the taller-growing ones. Cut off the spent flower heads leaving the green stalk until the leaves die down. For those to be planted in the garden: as soon as flowering finishes, tip the bulbs and their soil out of the pot and plant in the garden. Continue watering them until the foliage yellows then gradually lessen the amount until leaves are dead. Those to be kept in pots: allow soil to dry out as leaves wither. Repot *Lachenalia* in February using fresh soil mix and a little additional bone meal. *Hippeastrum* and Scarborough lilies prefer to be left in the same pots for two or three years. Simply replace a little of the top-soil with fresh soil mix and add slow-release fertiliser.

COMMON PROBLEMS Too much direct heat burns flowers. Mites may distort flower buds and foliage, and stain the base of the leaves.

Above ◆ **CROCUS**

Caladium

ELEPHANT'S EARS/ANGEL WINGS/HEART OF JESUS

These tropical, tuberous-rooted plants are grown for their vividly coloured foliage. They are not easily maintained unless high humidity and temperature can be provided. There are hundreds of hybrids whose arrow-shaped leaves vary in size and colours, ranging through silver, cream, white, pink, red and green, arranged in innumerable patterns. The flowers, usually only produced in glasshouse conditions, are insignificant and typical arum lily shape. When the cold weather comes the leaves die back, leaving a tuber in the ground from which, given the right conditions, new leaves will grow the following spring.

Below ◆ **CALADIUM**
Right ◆ **CALATHEA**
Below right ◆ **CALCEOLARIA**

LIGHT Filtered but bright light is needed to maintain the colourful pattern.
TEMPERATURE While growing and in leaf, a warm room not below 18°C.
WATERING AND FEEDING Keep the soil moist while the plant is actively growing but as the leaves die in autumn reduce the amount of water supplied. High nitrogen fertiliser tends to intensify the green colour of the leaves. Use a weak solution of liquid fertiliser only during active growth.
SPECIAL CARE A draught-free position and high humidity are essential during active growth. Remove leaves as they die. Keep dormant tuber in almost dry soil until repotting in spring.
COMMON PROBLEMS Collapse of leaves may be caused by draughts or dry atmosphere. Yellow leaves may result from overwatering in cool conditions.

Calathea

RATTLESNAKE PLANT/PEACOCK PLANT OR CATHEDRAL WINDOWS/ZEBRA PLANT

There are a number of these handsome tropical plants whose strongly patterned, long-stalked leaves spring from short central stems. Some have leaves up to 45 cm long which are narrow and undulating, such as the rattlesnake plant, Calathea lancifolia (often labelled C. insignis), one of the most easily grown of the group, while others are only half that length and oval in shape such as the peacock plant, C. makoyana. Patterns on the leaves vary from pale parallel lines to evenly placed elongated patches of darker colour or a contrasting band around the margin. The undersides of the leaves are often dull red or purple. The general appearance of these plants is similar to the well-known prayer plants (Maranta spp.) and the less common Ctenanthe spp.

LIGHT Medium light or heavily filtered bright light, for instance sunlight through a venetian blind.
TEMPERATURE A slightly warm room with a temperature around 20°C.

WATERING AND FEEDING

Keep the soil thoroughly moist during active growth but restrict watering during cold weather. Calathea species are greedy and should be fertilised regularly during the growing season. Use liquid or slow-release fertiliser and follow the maker's directions.

SPECIAL CARE Mist-spray or wipe the leaves with a damp cloth but do not use oil. Remove dead leaves. Keep the atmosphere humid especially in hot weather. Repot in late spring using a pot one size larger.

COMMON PROBLEMS Leaves curling upwards throughout the day may be caused by draughts, but if this occurs at night it could be normal. Too much light may cause leaf patterns to fade. Browning of leaf tips may be the result of too little water but large patches of discoloration could be the result of too much water in the dormant period.

Calceolaria hybrids

SLIPPER FLOWER/LADIES' PURSES/POUCH FLOWER OR WORT/POCKETBOOK

These colourful, bushy little plants with their strangely shaped pouched blooms are grown from seed annually and are usually available in the shops in early summer, as the flowers begin to open. They are not the easiest plants to keep in good condition indoors and once the flowers have faded after three or four weeks, like all annuals they should be discarded. The flowers are generally speckled in a contrasting colour and bloom in a range of yellows, oranges and reds.

LIGHT Bright light but not direct sunlight.
TEMPERATURE Cool.
WATERING AND FEEDING
Keep the soil moist at all times. No feeding necessary.
SPECIAL CARE A slightly humid atmosphere will increase the length of life. Avoid watering the leaves.
COMMON PROBLEMS Mildew.

Capsicum

ORNAMENTAL CHILLI/ ORNAMENTAL PEPPER/ ORNAMENTAL CANDLE PEPPER/ ORNAMENTAL HOT PEPPER

These short-lived perennials, usually treated as annuals, are available in autumn when their bright red and yellow miniature capsicum fruits attract attention. They are generally discarded when the fruits are spent but if they are pruned and put outside in a sheltered, sunny position until the following autumn they should bear fruit again. The small fruits may be rounded, cone shaped or long and thin and ripen into green, cream, yellow, orange, red or purple capsicums. Some varieties bear edible but very hot fruits; if children touch them they should keep their hands away from their mouth or eyes.

LIGHT Bright light with direct sunlight.
TEMPERATURE Normal room temperature.
WATERING AND FEEDING Keep the soil well watered but not water-logged.
SPECIAL CARE Tolerant of dry atmosphere.
COMMON PROBLEMS Leaves and fruit falling within a short space of time indicate insufficient light or dry soil.

Caryota

FISHTAIL PALM/JAGGERY PALM/WINE PALM/SAGO PALM

These highly ornamental plants are the only palms whose leaves are twice divided. Instead of being fan-shaped or split into feather-like fronds, each division of the large leaves is redivided, resulting in the ragged triangularsegments which give the palms their common name of fishtail. When mature these leaflets have a small sharp spine near the base. One species, the clustered fishtail palm, *Caryota*

Above ◆ **CAPSICUM**

Below ◆ **CARYOTA MITIS**

mitis, grows as a cluster of stems while the jaggery palm, *C. urens*, has only a single trunk. Given good conditions fishtail palms can be fast-growing in the garden but if confined to pots the growth rate is much slower and the ultimate height rarely more than 2.5 m.

LIGHT Filtered bright light.
TEMPERATURE A normal, warm room; fishtails will not tolerate cold conditions.
WATERING AND FEEDING
Keep the soil moist but not waterlogged. Following the maker's instructions feed with liquid or slow-release fertiliser only in warm weather.

SPECIAL CARE Fishtail palms like a draught-free position with increased humidity in hot weather. Repot in spring only every second or third year.

COMMON PROBLEMS Dry atmosphere encourages red spider which may cause browning of fronds. Watch for mealy bug.

Castanospermum Australe

BLACK BEAN/MORETON BAY CHESTNUT

A tall evergreen tree growing naturally along the coast of Queensland and northern New South Wales, the Moreton Bay chestnut, *Castanospermum australe*, makes a handsome indoor plant while young. Numbers of this species are usually planted in a small group to rapidly provide a well-filled container. The trunks are grey and the foliage glossy. The leaves, 30-40 cm long, are made up of narrow, oval leaflets arranged on each side of a central rib; they are light green when young but mature to a rich, dark shade. The bright orange flowers and large seed pods, so conspicuous in garden plants, are not normally produced indoors.

LIGHT Bright with some direct sunlight.

TEMPERATURE Normal room temperatures throughout the year but prefers a warm position.

WATERING AND FEEDING Keep the soil moist but water more sparingly in cooler conditions. Use liquid or slow-release fertiliser, high in nitrogen to encourage leaf growth, from spring to early autumn.

SPECIAL CARE These are hard, easily grown plants which are generally discarded after 2-3 years as by then they are often too large to keep indoors. Keep the foliage clean with a damp cloth but avoid leaf gloss preparations. Repot in spring if necessary.

COMMON PROBLEMS If the atmosphere is dry, red spider mite may be a problem. A sudden drop in temperature may cause leaf-fall.

Ceropegia Woodii

CHAIN OF HEARTS

Once established, these small trailing succulents are not difficult to maintain. The long stems, which have been known to reach over 2 m in length, grow from a rounded storage organ on

Right ◆ **CASTANOSPERMUM AUSTRALA**
Below ◆ **CEROPEGIA WOODII**

the surface of the soil. The pairs of heart-shaped, grey-green leaves are heavily splashed with silver and have dull purple lower surfaces. The leaves are scattered along the slender pendant stems, as are small storage tubers which may be used for propagation. Tubular purple flowers appear in late summer and autumn.

LIGHT Bright light and some direct sunlight will strengthen the colouring in the leaves. Too much shade will increase the length of stem between the pairs of leaves.

TEMPERATURE Normal room temperature.

WATERING AND FEEDING From spring to early autumn keep the soil just moist, then restrict watering until the soil is almost dry. Use standard fertilisers sparingly.

SPECIAL CARE If growing from a tuber, several weeks will elapse before any top growth emerges. These plants tolerate dry atmosphere. Repot in pring only when roots have filled the pot.

COMMON PROBLEMS None.

Chamaecereus Sylvestrii

PEANUT CACTUS

This free-flowering, prostrate cactus is very easily grown and quickly increases in size. The pale cylindrical stems, up to 15 cm long, form closely packed clumps and have longitudinal ribs and clusters of small spines typical of many cacti. The numerous short-lived scarlet flowers, about 2.5 cm in diameter, appear in early summer over a period of two or three weeks. Hybrid forms of the peanut cactus have flowers in colours ranging through yellows, oranges, reds and purples.

LIGHT Direct sunlight.

TEMPERATURE While in active growth the plant prefers normal room temperature. A much cooler position in winter will ensure a dormant spell.

WATERING AND FEEDING Allow top of soil to dry out between waterings during growing periods. While the plant is dormant, the soil can be completely dry. Apply slow-release fertiliser early in the growing season.

SPECIAL CARE Prefers a normal to dry atmosphere and a rest during cold weather. Repot in spring when the plant becomes too crowded.

COMMON PROBLEMS Straggly growth with spindly stems results from insufficient light and sun.

Chamaedorea

(SYN. *NEANTHE*, *COLLINIA*)

PARLOUR PALM OR GOOD-LUCK PALM/WALKING STICK PALM/FISHTAIL PALM

These attractive and elegant palms adapt well to indoor conditions and will grow to maturity in containers. The parlour palm, *Chamaedorea elegans*, once known as *Neanthe bella* and *Collinia elegans*, has a single stem which may eventually reach 2 m but usually grows to around 1 m in a pot. In some specimens, aerial roots grow from the trunk. The feather fronds have deep green segments and the upright flowering branches bear small orange fruits which become black with age. As these plants are grown from seed collected in the wild there is some variation amongst them. The taller growing bamboo palm, *Chamaedorea erumpens*, has several stems bearing drooping leaves with broad leaflets. Coral-red flowering branches carry black fruit.

LIGHT Bright but filtered.

TEMPERATURE Tolerates any normal room temperature but prefers a temperature of around 20°C.

WATERING AND FEEDING Keep the soil thoroughly moist while the plant is actively growing but reduce water in the winter allowing the top half of the soil to dry out. Use half-strength liquid fertiliser

Above ♦ **CHAMAECEREUS SYLVESTRII**
Below ♦ **CHAMAEDOREA ELEGANS**

during active period.

SPECIAL CARE These palms prefer a humid atmosphere. Wipe fronds with a damp cloth to remove dust.

COMMON PROBLEMS Brown tips on young fronds could indicate in- sufficient water when frond was forming. Large brown areas could be caused by sudden exposure to hot sun. Watch for scale and red spider.

Chamaerops Humilus

EUROPEAN FAN PALM/DWARF FAN PALM

This hardy, slow-growing palm comes from the Mediterranean coast. As an indoor plant it usually has a single stem which, as the plant ages, becomes covered with grey fibres left behind when the leaf stalks fall. The grey-green, fan-shaped leaves are folded into stiff narrow segments and the leaf stalks have sharp spines along their edges. The plant grows to about 1.5 m in a container, spreading out into a rounded hush. Flowers and fruit are not generally produced.

LIGHT Well-lit position with a little direct sun if possible. Needs less light in winter.

TEMPERATURE A warm room during the growing season with cooler conditions in winter.

WATERING AND FEEDING Keep the soil thoroughly moist in warm weather but reduce watering in winter when the plant is resting. Use liquid or slow-release fertiliser following the maker's instructions.

SPECIAL CARE Use a soil based potting mix and repot into a large container every two years.

COMMON PROBLEMS Spindly growth indicates too little light. Watch for scale, mealy bug and red spider.

Above ◆ **CHAMAEROPS HUMILIS**

Chlorophytum Comosum 'Vittatum'

SPIDER PLANT/RIBBON PLANT/WALKING ANTHERICUM

This hardy, fast-growing plant is most popular in its variegated forms, with long, arching, green and cream or white striped leaves. During warm weather, thin creamy-yellow stems emerge from the clump of mature leaves and grow to about 50-60 cm. At the tips appear small white flowers and, a little later, tufts of small leaves which develop into young plants. The weight causes the stems to arch over which, coupled with the pendulous leaves, makes the spider plant ideal for hanging baskets. Once the plantlets have grown roots they may be cut off and grown separately.

LIGHT Bright light with cool sunlight.

TEMPERATURE Spider plants tolerate a wide range of normal room temperatures.

WATERING AND FEEDING Keep the soil thoroughly moist in summer and just damp in winter. Feed during warm months with liquid or slow-release fertiliser following maker's instructions.

SPECIAL CARE Remove old and discoloured leaves. Turn the pot if growth is lopsided. Repot in spring when the roots fill the pot.

COMMON PROBLEMS Spider plants appear to be sensitive to chemicals such as chlorine or fluoride in the water which causes the tips of the leaves to turn brown.

Left ◆ **CHLOROPHYTUM**
Above ◆ **CHRYSANTHEMUM 'SHANTUNG'**
Below Left ◆ **CHRYSALIDOCARPUS**

Chrysalidocarpus Lutescens

GOLDEN CANE PALM/YELLOW PALM/BUTTERFLY PALM/GOLDEN FEATHER PALM

This elegant feather-leafed palm with its suckering habit makes a fine indoor plant for a big tub in a warm room. Although fast-growing in the garden, these palms are considerably slower in containers. The bright yellow-green stems are prominently ringed like bamboo canes and the young suckers cluster close around the base. Each stem carries only a few arching fronds which are divided into narrow leaflets but several stems together produce a full plant.

LIGHT Filtered bright light.

TEMPERATURE A warm room in the growing season but the golden cane palm will tolerate cooler winter conditions.

WATERING AND FEEDING Keep the soil thoroughly moist in warm weather but restrict the water supply in winter. Feed during spring and summer.

SPECIAL CARE Keep the leaves free of dust using a damp cloth. Avoid leaf gloss preparations or oil. Repotting every other year is usually sufficient.

COMMON PROBLEMS Brown tips to the leaves may be the result of insufficient moisture in the soil.

Chrysanthemum

CHRYSANTHEMUM

Ordinary autumn-flowering chrysanthemums are garden plants which come into bloom as the days grow shorter. However modern nursery techniques, using shaded glass houses and dwarfing chemicals, have produced small, bushy, flower-covered plants for use as indoor decorations at any time of the year. These chrysanthemums are best bought when the first flowers are opening so they may be enjoyed for as long as possible before they are discarded. To keep these potted plants looking healthy, they must be given the right conditions. If planted out in the garden when they have finished flowering, given time to adjust, they will behave as normal garden plants, but because they will be freed from dwarfing compounds, they will grow taller.

LIGHT Bright but no direct sunlight.

TEMPERATURE A cool position will lengthen their life.

WATERING AND FEEDING Keep the soil moist, no feeding is necessary. 35

SPECIAL CARE A slightly humid atmosphere, especially during a hot dry spell.

COMMON PROBLEMS There should be none if the plant is healthy when bought.

Above ◆ **CISSUS RHOMBIFOLIA**
'ELLEN DANICA'
Right ◆ **CISSUS RHOMBIFOLIA**

Cissus

KANGAROO VINE/KANGAROO IVY/GRAPE IVY

These fast-growing trailing and climbing evergreens are amongst the most easy-going of indoor plants as they accept a wider range of light intensity than many others. The Australian native kangaroo vine or kangaroo ivy, *Cissus antarctica*, has tendril climbing stems which may be as long as 3 m and are easily trained up a support or left to trail from a hanging basket. The heavily-veined, glossy oval leaves are about 10 cm long with widely toothed margins. The grape ivy, *C. rhombifolia* (sometimes labelled *Rhoicissus rhomboidea*), is even more tolerant of its conditions than the kangaroo vine. The stems are longer and more vigorous, climbing by means of forked tendrils, and the shining dark green leaves are made up of three leaflets with widely spaced serrations along the margins. Young leaves are covered with pale down. The recently introduced variety *Cissus rhombifolia* 'Ellen Danica' has larger leaflets than the species, almost circular in shape with deeply lobed edges.

LIGHT Accepts a wide range but prefers bright filtered light, not direct sunlight.

TEMPERATURE A normal warm room temperature most of the year, with a rest in cooler surroundings during winter.

WATERING AND FEEDING
Water thoroughly but allow soil on top to dry before watering again. Less water is required in winter. Feed during the growing season with liquid or slow-release fertiliser following the maker's instructions.

SPECIAL CARE If long trailers are not wanted, pinch back to produce a bushier plant. Tie the stems to supports to help train them upwards. Prune old plants fairly heavily before repotting in spring.

COMMON PROBLEMS
Watch for red spider.

Clerodendron Thomsonae

BLEEDING HEARTS

A twining evergreen climber, bleeding hearts, *Clerodendron thomsonae* (once known as *C. balfouri*), needs some support in order to display its flowers in spring. The deep green leaves are slightly wrinkled and provide a good background for the large hanging clusters of angular, white, heart-shaped bracts and their emergent scarlet flowers.

LIGHT Bright filtered light but no direct sunlight.

TEMPERATURE Normal warm room temperature, not below 10°C in winter.

WATERING AND FEEDING Water well during the warm months but more sparingly in winter. Do not let water accumulate in the saucer. Feed with liquid or slow-release fertiliser, following the maker's instructions, from spring to early autumn.

SPECIAL CARE Mist-spray or provide a humid atmosphere especially during hot dry weather. Old branches should be pruned back hard in spring and repotting, if required, carried out at the same time.

COMMON PROBLEMS Premature leaf-fall may be caused by a sudden drop in temperature.

Codiaeum Variegatum

CROTON

These flamboyant plants are grown for their colourful leaves which come in a great variety of shapes and colour combinations but are all cultivars of the same species, *Codiaeum variegatum*. Most are bushy shrubs no more than 1 m in height, although almost as wide as they are high. The slender spikes of small, greenish flowers are insignificant but the glossy, leathery leaves are particularly striking. Shapes vary from simple ovals to narrow straps and some are divided into lobes, while the colour may be spotted, blotched, netted or patterned in white and shades of yellows, oranges and reds. The young foliage often differs from the mature leaves.

LIGHT Bright light, including direct sunlight.

TEMPERATURE Normal to warm room temperature, but not cool conditions.

WATERING AND FEEDING Keep soil thoroughly damp but not waterlogged during growing period. Reduce water in cooler weather until the soil is barely moist. Feed regularly through the growing season with liquid fertiliser following maker's directions.

SPECIAL CARE Crotons need a humid atmosphere. Mist-spray in dry weather and wipe leaves with a damp cloth but avoid leaf gloss preparations. Repot annually into a pot one size larger.

COMMON PROBLEMS Premature leaf-drop may be caused by too little light or a sudden lowering of temperature. Watch for red spider.

Left ◆ CLERODENDRON THOMSONAE
Below ◆ CODIAEUM VARIEGATUM VAR. PICTUM
Bottom ◆ CODIAEUM VARIEGATUM

Coleus Blumei

COLEUS/FLAME NETTLE/PAINTED LEAVES

These fast-growing plants with their multi-coloured leaves are true perennials but are often treated as annuals and discarded when cold weather causes the foliage to drop. Although they are all descendants of *Coleus blumei* there are many different colour combinations and some variety of shape in the soft leaves. Among the more common varieties are cream and green; dull brownish-red edged with yellow, or green with a wide central stripe of cerise. Given the right conditions, coleus can make bushy little plants up to 60 cm tall, while the trailing varieties will soon fill a hanging basket.

LIGHT Bright light with some direct sunlight but not too much or the colours will fade.

TEMPERATURE A warm room all the year round.

WATERING AND FEEDING Keep the soil well-watered and feed with liquid or slow-release fertiliser in spring and summer.

SPECIAL CARE Coleus need a humid atmosphere, especially at higher temperatures. Pinch back new growth to develop a bushy shape and remove flower spikes well before seeds appear. Repot during the growing season if plants are bought in small containers.

COMMON PROBLEMS Leaf-drop can be caused by low temperatures and insufficient water, especially in warm weather. Both a lack of light and excessive direct sun may fade the colours. Watch for red spider if the atmosphere is dry.

Above ◆ **COLEUS BLUMEI**

Columnea

GOLDFISH PLANT/COLUMN FLOWER

These plants are most attractive in hanging baskets, with their orange-red flowers scattered down long stems. In some forms, the branches are arching whereas in others they trail vertically downwards but the small, often hairy, leaves are always arranged in opposite pairs along their length. The long-lasting, tubular flowers come in shades of orange or red and their general shape gives the plants their common name of goldfish plants. Although these are very decorative plants, they are not the easiest to keep in good condition because they need warmth and high humidity all the year round.

LIGHT Bright but filtered.

TEMPERATURE A warm room around 20°C.

WATERING AND FEEDING The soil should be kept barely moist as these plants rot if overwatered. Even less water should be given when the plant is resting.

Left ◆ **COLUMNEA**

Above ◆ **CORDYLINE AUSTRALIS**

Feed with a weak solution of high-phosphate liquid fertiliser only during active growth.

SPECIAL CARE Mist-spray once a day with room-temperature water and keep the humidity high. Repot when roots fill the container.

COMMON PROBLEMS Lack of flowers. To initiate flowering, the plants need long nights and cooler temperature but no lower then 13°C.

Cordyline

TREE OF KINGS/NEW ZEALAND CABBAGE TREE/GOOD LUCK PLANT/HAWAIIAN TI/BABY TI/REDEDGE/PALM LILY/GIANT OR FOUNTAIN DRACAENA

Grown for their beautiful foliage, these plants are often confused with *Draecenas* and may be called by that name. The New Zealand cabbage tree or fountain dracaena, *Cordyline australis*, is a hardy, easily managed plant even when grown indoors. The tough green leaves, up to 90 cm long, are arranged on a single stem, the lower ones drying and falling as they age and the new ones emerging at the tip.

There are also two varieties which have coloured leaves, one with green and white striped foliage, the other, a slower-growing and smaller variety, with purple-bronze markings on its leaves. The Hawaiian Ti or good luck plant, *C. terminalis*, is not quite so hardy. The leaves are much more strongly coloured in rich red, bronze and green and there are a number of differently coloured varieties. Flowers rarely develop on cordylines grown in pots.

LIGHT Bright with a little direct sunlight for the New Zealand cabbage tree but only filtered strong light for the Hawaiian Ti.

TEMPERATURE Normal room temperatures but the New Zealand cabbage tree tolerates lower temperatures.

WATERING AND FEEDING Keep the soil well-watered but not waterlogged. Reduce the amount in winter until the soil is just moist. Use fertiliser only in spring and summer.

SPECIAL CARE Wipe the leaves with a damp cloth but avoid commercial leaf gloss. Spraying leaves of the Hawaiian Ti may cause spotting. If possible put the New Zealand cabbage tree outside for a few weeks in late summer. Repot annually in spring.

COMMON PROBLEMS Browning of the leaf margins may be caused by fluoride in the water.

Crassula

SILVER JADE PLANT/CHINESE JADE/PROPELLER PLANT

This large group of succulents varies widely in size, habit and requirements. Fortunately the species commonly cultivated are tolerant and adaptable. They range through prostrate forms, such as *Crassula rupestris* with small, thick, blue-grey leaves; trailing types such as *C. marginalis rubra* whose strings of reddish, heart-shaped leaves will spill attractively from hanging baskets; and bushy varieties such as the well-known *C. arborescens* (which grows to 1 m in height with rounded grey-green leaves edged in red) and the slightly smaller silver jade plant, *C. argentea*, whose fleshy, rounded leaves are glossy, dark green. With the exception of the propeller plant, *C. falcata*, which has large heads of orange-red flowers in summer, most of the *Crassula* species have small flowers in pale colours.

LIGHT Bright with full sun especially for flower production.

TEMPERATURE Normal room temperatures most of the year, but a cool resting period in winter is necessary for continued good growth.

WATERING AND FEEDING From spring to autumn keep the soil just moist allowing the pot to become half dry between waterings. In winter reduce water until soil is only barely damp. Apply slow-release fertiliser in spring following maker's directions.

SPECIAL CARE Like other succulents these plants prefer a dry atmosphere. Spraying with some pesticides can damage the plant. Repot every other year if necessary but these plants are happy slightly pot-bound.

COMMON PROBLEMS Elongated, lanky growth is probably caused by insufficient light.

Top Left ◆ **CRASSULA**
Left ◆ **CROSSANDRA**
Above ◆ **CTENANTHE LUBBERSIANA**

Crossandra Infundibuliformis
(SYN. C. UNDULIFOLIA)
FIRECRACKER FLOWER

This small, bright-flowering plant thrives in a warm, humid atmosphere and may reach 45-60 cm in height. The shiny, dark green leaves, up to 12 cm long, have conspicuously depressed veins and the orange-pink flowers appear in spring and summer arranged on a narrow spike, pushed out between green bracts which give the spike an angular appearance. Because of their comparatively small size and love of humid conditions, firecracker flowers grow well planted in a group, either with other humidity lovers or amongst their own kind.

LIGHT Bright but filtered.

TEMPERATURE Warm conditions all through the year.

WATERING AND FEEDING From spring to late summer keep the soil moist allowing the top to dry out between waterings. In cold weather reduce the amount of water. Use liquid fertiliser high in phosphorus (P) during spring and summer.

SPECIAL CARE Keep the humidity high but avoid mist-spraying on to the flowers. Repot annually if the plant is growing well.

COMMON PROBLEMS Spots on leaves may be caused by cold water; yellowing of foliage is probably the result of overwatering.

Ctenanthe

NEVER-NEVER PLANT

These erect, leafy perennials, growing up to 60-90 cm, are closely related to prayer plants and other species of *Maranta*. As the plant matures, the narrow cluster of long-stalked leaves forms a stem which begins branching and carrying more leaves at intervals. The more popular species have variegated leaves, those of *Ctenanthe lubbersiana*, one of the easiest to grow, patterned in irregularly shaded bands of mid-green and yellow with pale green undersides, and those of *C. oppenheimiana* 'Tricolor' marked with more distinct stripes of silver on dark green with purple undersides. The flowers of *Ctenanthe* species are insignificant.

LIGHT Bright but filtered. Too light light will reduce the variegations.

TEMPERATURE Normal room temperature. C.o. 'Tricolor' prefers a warm position.

WATERING AND FEEDING Keep the soil moist in the growing season but do not allow the plant to stand in water as the roots rot easily. Keep the soil only just damp in winter. Feed with liquid or slow-release fertiliser in spring and summer.

SPECIAL CARE A humid atmosphere is important to these plants, especially C.o. 'Tricolor'. Keep the leaves dust free with a damp cloth. Repot in spring using a wide container to allow the shallow roots to spread.

COMMON PROBLEMS Direct sunlight may cause the leaves to curl up. Poor growth may be the result of low humidity.

Cycas Revoluta

CYCADS/JAPANESE SAGO PALM

Members of a very ancient plant family developed long before flowering plants, Cycads are so slow-growing that only one new leaf may be produced in a year. Although usually seen with a single stem, the stout trunk may branch at ground level. The feather-like fronds have closely crowded, narrow, dark greenish-brown leaflets and short stalks armed with spines. Erect at first, they gradually arch out until they droop when mature.

LIGHT Sunlight or very strong light is essential for growth.

TEMPERATURE Cycads thrive in a very wide range of temperatures and are resistant to the cold.

WATERING AND FEEDING Keep the soil moist but not wet throughout the year. Feed during the spring and summer with liquid or slowrelease fertiliser according to the maker's instructions.

SPECIAL CARE Apart from needing sufficient light, the sago palm is easy-going and does not require a humid atmosphere. Repot only when plant fills container.

COMMON PROBLEMS Watch for scale and mealy bug above and below the soil.

Cyclamen hybrids

CYCLAMEN

The many varieties of cyclamen now available are the result of nearly 200 years of plant breeding. Over the years the size and colour range of the flowers was increased but the perfume produced by the original wild species was lost. Some of the more recently introduced small forms have recaptured this delicate scent, although the giant ones have not. Some cyclamen have plain green leaves but in many the foliage is attractively patterned in silver. The flowers, with reflexed petals, plain or frilled, may be white, deep red or any of a wide range of pinks and mauves. The fleshy stalks of both leaves and flowers spring from a flattened, bulb-like storage organ, often called a dorm, which is highly susceptible to rot, and should therefore be partly exposed above the soil and kept dry when watering. The plants are usually available in early winter when the first buds open into flowers. They should continue flowering for 6-8 weeks or more and then remain decorative for another month or longer until the leaves begin to wither and turn yellow. There are so many opinions about

Left ◆ **CYCAS REVOLUTA**

growing cyclamen perhaps it is easier to remember the advice of a very experienced grower: keep the soil on the dry side and the plant in a cool well-lit position.

LIGHT Good light is important and a little cool sunlight will not harm them.

TEMPERATURE An even temperature no higher than 16°-18°C is best. Good ventilation but no draughts.

WATERING AND FEEDING Water from below by standing in a bowl of water or pour the water carefully over the side of the pot making sure the top of the corm remains dry. While the plant is actively growing keep the soil moist but once it is flowering the growth slows and therefore less water is required to maintain sufficient moisture. Continue watering when flowering has finished for as long as the leaves remain healthy as this is when the plant in building next year's blooms. Once the leaves start to yellow, gradually reduce water and allow the pot to dry off. While the plant is growing, feed with liquid or slow-release fertiliser following maker's directions.

SPECIAL CARE Cyclamen dislike a dry atmosphere and double potting is a good way to increase the humidity. If mist-spraying the leaves avoid spotting the flowers. When removing the spent flowers or yellow leaves, pull the stalk away from the corm, or the remaining stalk may cause rotting. After the leaves have died down put the pot in a cool place, keeping the soil barely moist, until new leaves appear. Then repot in a container one size larger, keeping the corm well above soil level, and restart watering. Once roots form begin fertilising.

COMMON PROBLEMS Yellowing leaves may be caused by insufficient or excessive water. Sudden changes in temperature, even those caused when transferring the plant from the shop to your home, will cause the plant to collapse. High temperatures and a dry atmosphere will shrivel flower buds.

Top Right ◆ **CYCLAMEN**

Right ◆ **CYCLAMEN HEDERIFOLIUM**

Cymbidium hybrids

ORCHIDS

These orchids with their sprays of blooms ranging from greenish-yellows to purplish-pinks are usually available in general nurseries in late winter and spring. If they are bought when first blooms open they should last for at least six weeks. After flowering finishes the old stem should be removed and the plant could be put outside, or if it can be kept in a fresh, airy but out-of-the-way spot, it could remain inside. To produce flowers the following season orchids need some dappled sunlight after flowering and a cool spell in winter.

LIGHT Good but no direct sunlight while in flower. After flowering, dappled sunlight will encourage the formation of the next season's flowers.

TEMPERATURE Normal room temperature from spring to autumn but lower (about 10°C) during winter.

WATERING AND FEEDING Keep the soil moist but allow the top to dry out between waterings during growing season. While resting restrict watering further. Fertilise only during the growing season.

SPECIAL CARE Orchids need a humid atmosphere when the weather is warm. Be careful not to overwater or to leave the pot standing in water or the roots will rot. Repot immediately after flowering only if the plant completely fills the pot.

COMMON PROBLEMS Lack of flowers may be caused by insufficient sunlight and absence of cold spell in winter. Watch for red spider mites, scale and mealy bugs.

Above ◆ **CYMBIDIUM SAYONARIA**
Below ◆ **MINI-CYMBIDIUM**

Cyperus

**UMBRELLA PALM/DWARF
UMBRELLA PLANT**

These are grass-like plants notable for their preference for standing in water. Tolerant of a wide range of temperature and light intensities, there are three forms commonly grown indoors. The broad-leafed umbrella plant, *Cyperus albostriatus* (sometimes seen under its old name *C. diffusus*), has heads of long, radiating leaf-like bracts and grass-like flowers held on thin upright stems which are generally less than 1 m in height. Long narrow leaves cluster around the base of the stems. The umbrella plant, *C. alternifolius*, is similar but the bracts are much narrower rather like the ribs of an umbrella, and the stems may be more than 1 m in height. A shorter and smaller form the dwarf umbrella plant, *C. alternifolius* 'Gracilis', is also available.

LIGHT Will accept direct sunlight or shaded positions.

TEMPERATURE Normal room temperature even down to10°C in winter.

WATERING AND FEEDING The umbrella plant and its dwarf form cannot be overwatered when actively growing, but should not have the whole pot submerged in water as the roots may rot. A saucer of water is ideal. The broad-leafed umbrella plant is also water-loving but some growers find standing in water causes root rot, so choose to keep the soil thoroughly moist. Fertilise during growing period.

SPECIAL CARE A well-ventilated room but humid atmosphere. Repot when plant fills the container.

COMMON PROBLEMS Lack of new stems could be the result of too little light. Browning at the tips of the leaf-bracts will occur if the atmosphere is dry.

Top ◆ **CYPERUS ALTERNIFOLIUS**
Right ◆ **CYRTOMIUM FALCATUM**

Cyrtomium Falcatum

HOLLY FERN

This popular Japanese fern has become naturalised in parts of Australia and, as the common name suggests, has glossy dark green leaflets with spiky margins. The thick creeping stems which from the base of the plant give rise to many upright fronds from 40-60 cm long whose short stalks are covered with coarse scales. This hardy fern tolerates cool temperatures and medium light.

LIGHT Medium or bright filtered.

TEMPERATURE Normal room temperature and down to10°C or so in winter.

WATERING AND FEEDING Keep the soil moist but allow it to dry out a little on top when temperatures are low. Feed in spring and summer with half-strength fertiliser unless maker gives specific instructions for ferns.

SPECIAL CARE Like other ferns the holly fern prefers a humid atmosphere and air unpolluted by cooking fumes, especially as temperatures rise. Double potting is particularly suitable. When fronds age they may be cut back to ground level in late winter and a new crop will soon be produced. Repot at the same time if the roots have filled the pot.

COMMON PROBLEMS Browning of mature fronds could be natural aging or could be caused by lack of moisture or humidity. Watch for scale.

Davallia

HARE'S FOOT FERN/DEER'S FOOT FERN/SQUIRREL'S FOOT OR BALL FERN

There are some Australian natives among this group of ferns, all of which have fronds rising from thick creeping stems covered with soft furry scales, which accounts for the common name. The scales may be black, brown, grey or silver. The roughly triangular fronds are deeply divided and lacy and are carried on long stalks, the whole leaf being 20-60 cm in length. The Australian *Davallia pyxidata*, the native hare's foot fern, is very easily grown and like all these ferns makes an excellent plant for a hanging basket.

LIGHT Medium light and no direct sun.
TEMPERATURE Normal room temperature including cooler winter temperatures.
WATERING AND FEEDING Keep the soil moist but not waterlogged during the growing period; reduce the amount of water applied in winter. Feed with half strength fertiliser from early spring to early autumn while plants are making new fronds.
SPECIAL CARE Unlike most, the hare's foot fern will tolerate a dry atmosphere. Repot in early spring if creeping stems have covered the surface of the pot.
COMMON PROBLEMS Premature death of fronds may be caused by lack of moisture or cold temperatures. Watch for scale.

Dichorisandra Reginae

QUEEN'S SPIDERWORT

When the queen's spiderwort was first exhibited in 1890 it was so admired by the Queen of the Belgians that it was named after her. This handsome, rather slow-growing relative of the wandering Jew, *Tradescantia fluminensis*, is somewhat similar to it in appearance but the waxy, dark green leaves are slightly bigger, up to 13 cm long, and widely striped and speckled in silver with deep purple lower surfaces. The succulent stems are upright but may require staking to support them as they sometimes grow to 50-60 cm in height. Three-petalled lavender flowers are produced in late summer but are of little importance as the queen's spiderwort is grown for its handsome foliage.

Left ◆ **DAVALLIA**
Above ◆ **DICHORISANDRA REGINAE**

LIGHT Medium.
TEMPERATURE Tolerates normal room temperature but will grow all year if kept in a warm position.
WATERING AND FEEDING Water enough to moisten the soil thoroughly then allow the top centimetre or so to dry out before watering again. If the temperature falls, water more sparingly. Use liquid or slow-release fertiliser, following the maker's instructions, while the plant is growing actively.
SPECIAL CARE A humid atmosphere is important. Repot whenever roots fill the container.
COMMON PROBLEMS Foliage browning is probably the result of dry atmosphere.

Dieffenbachia

DUMB CANE/DUMB PLANT/TUFTROOT

These tropical shrubby plants with their thick, upright stems and large variegated leaves are amongst the most popular of indoor plants although they do not respond well to the dry atmosphere of many heated buildings. The long stalks bear large green leaves from 25-60 cm long which may be striped, spotted or splashed with white, cream or yellow, usually with a conspicuous central vein. As in other members of the arum family, the flowers of dumb canes are insignificant. These plants have poisonous sap which can cause irritation to the eyes and mouth and may paralyse the vocal cords.

LIGHT Bright but filtered except in winter when cool sunlight is beneficial.

TEMPERATURE Warm room; even in winter the temperature should not drop below 10°-12°C.

WATERING AND FEEDING Keep the soil moist, allowing the top 1-2 cm to dry out between waterings. If the temperature can be kept warm all year round the dumb canes will continue to grow. Feed while actively growing.

SPECIAL CARE Keep the atmosphere humid. Mist-spray and wipe the leaves clean with a damp cloth but avoid commercial leaf gloss preparations. Remove old leaves as they wither. Repot annually in spring.

COMMON PROBLEMS Fading variegations may be caused by insufficient light. Collapse of foliage may result from too much water when the temperature is low.

Above ◆ **DIEFFENBACNIA AMOENA**
Top Right ◆ **DIZYGOTHECA ELEGANTISSIMA**
Right ◆ **DOODIA CAUDATA**

Dizygotheca Elegantissma

FALSE OR FINGER ARALIA

This delicate looking shrub has reddish-brown leaves when young, composed of about ten narrow radiating leaflets with saw toothed margins which change to dark green as they mature. They spread out from the tips of long stalks which, like the main stem, are speckled with white. While it remains indoors in a container the false aralia will grow no more than about 1.5 m in height but if planted out in the garden it will become a small tree up to 8 m tall with much larger, coarser leaves.

LIGHT Bright but filtered light.

TEMPERATURE A warm position is important; even in winter it should not drop below 15°C.

WATERING AND FEEDING Allow the top half of the soil to dry out between watering even when the plant is actively growing. Feed with liquid or slow-release fertiliser during growing season, following maker's directions.

SPECIAL CARE High humidity is essential. The false aralia needs good ventilation but not draughts. Repot in spring only when necessary, usually every second or third year.

COMMON PROBLEMS Prone to attack by scale.

Doodia

RASP FERNS

The hardy rasp ferns, *Doodia*, which take their common name from their rather coarse, harsh foliage, grow indoors very easily. The fronds are similar in shape to those of the common fishbone ferns, being long and narrow and divided into thin, strap-shaped segments. They spring from wiry, black creeping stems. The prickly rasp fern, Doodia aspera, has pale green upright fronds which are, surprisingly, bright pink when young. The small rasp fern, D. caudata, is a variable plant but usually has spreading or weeping fronds about 30 cm long, the segments often curling upwards.

LIGHT Medium to bright.

TEMPERATURE Growing naturally in a wide range of temperatures from north Queensland to eastern Victoria, rasp ferns will tolerate most normal room temperatures.

WATERING AND FEEDING Keep the soil moist but not sodden and feed with half-strength liquid fertiliser while actively growing.

SPECIAL CARE Avoid draughty positions. Repot in spring if the roots fill the pot.

COMMON PROBLEMS Watch for scale and mealy bug.

Dracaena

SPOTTED LEAF DRACAENA/GOLD DUST DRACAENA/DRAGON TREE

There are many varieties of these upright plants which are popular for their lush, strikingly marked foliage. They are often confused with *Cordyline* species. The differences are mainly botanical but on the whole dracaenas have yellow roots and cordylines white. The leaves on young plants spring directly from the thick trunk, while on older plants the trunk may branch. New leaves at the tip are erect when young but arch out as they mature and finally droop before they die and fall off. Thus as the plant grows, the lower part of the stem becomes bare. The height of a plant varies with the variety as do the coloured stripes on the leaves which may be white, red or yellow. Amongst the most popular are the varieties of *Dracaena deremensis* which may reach

1.2 m in height and have 5 cm wide leaves striped in white. *D. fragrans* varieties grow no taller than *D. deremensis*, but make much bushier plants as their leaves are twice as large and striped either in gold (*D. fragrans* 'Massangeana') or white (*D. fragrans* 'Lindenii'). The popular Chinese 'happy plants' belong to this group. *D. marginata* 'Tricolor' can easily grow to 3 m, the long bare stem topped by a bunch of 60 cm long but very narrow leaves striped in deep pink, cream and green. The spotted leaf or gold dust dracaena, *D. surculosa*, has quite a different habit from these and is a little more exacting in its requirements. Instead of a single thick trunk this plant makes several slender stems which form a bushy plant of just over 50 cm in height with dark green oval leaves heavily spotted with

Above ◆ **DRACAENA DEREMENSIS**

deep yellow, which fade as they age. The gold dust dracaena is quickly affected by cool winter conditions and is susceptible to root rot if the soil is too wet.

LIGHT Bright light but no direct sunlight.

TEMPERATURE Normal room temperature but not below 15°C in winter.

WATERING AND FEEDING Keep the soil moist but not sodden while the plant is making new leaves then allow the top of the soil to dry out between waterings. Do not allow to stand in water. Feed only while the plant is actively growing.

SPECIAL CARE A humid atmosphere is needed. Mist-spray the foliage in hot dry weather and keep the leaves dust free with a damp cloth. Avoid leaf shine preparations. Repot only when roots fill the container: the larger the leaf the sooner this will be.

COMMON PROBLEMS Leaf-drop or loss of colour in leaves of *D. surculosa* may be caused by insufficient light. Browning along leaf margins may be the result of too much fluoride in the water.

Echeveria

PAINTED LADY

This group of succulents comes in a great variety of forms ranging from stemless mat-forming rosettes of fleshy leaves to trailing varieties or small bushy shrubs. The foliage may have a smooth surface with a waxy finish or it may be covered in fine hairs but in all cases it is easily damaged by careless handling. The bell-shaped flowers in yellows, oranges and reds appear in late winter, spring or summer at the top of long flexible stems which rise from between the leaves.

LIGHT Bright, including direct sunlight.

TEMPERATURE Normal room temperatures. Cooler conditions in winter, down to 12°C, induce a beneficial resting period.

WATERING AND FEEDING
From spring to autumn let at least half the soil dry out between waterings. In winter, further reduce the amount. Feed only during the growing season.

SPECIAL CARE Keep the water away from the leaves as it may mark or rot them. These plants prefer a dry atmosphere. Repot annually in spring.

COMMON PROBLEMS The rosette should be tight; loose growth is probably caused by insufficient light. Shrivelling leaves may result from lack of water.

Episcia Dianthiflora

LACE FLOWER/FLAME VIOLET

Provided it can have warmth and humidity the trailing habit of this little plant makes it ideal for hanging baskets. As the slender stems grow they develop small clusters of leaves at the joints and, if resting on soil, these will take root. The soft, mid-green leaves are covered with fine hairs. In summer the comparatively large white flowers appear, consisting of tubes which open out into five deeply fringed lobes. Other *Episcia* species have copper, bronze or variegated leaves and red flowers. All require the same conditions.

LIGHT Bright with some cool sunlight.

TEMPERATURE Warm, above 15°C at all times.

WATERING AND FEEDING
Although these plants require moist soil, overwatering will lead to rotting. Less water is needed as the temperature falls. Feed with weak fertiliser through spring and summer.

SPECIAL CARE Humid atmosphere is necessary for a healthy plant. Nipping back the runners after flowering will induce larger leaves and bigger flowers. Some growers think the plant should not be moved when it is resting as a change in temperature can be harmful. Repot just before active growth

starts only if roots fill the pot. Use a wide rather than deep container to accommodate the shallow spreading root system.

COMMON PROBLEMS Insufficient light may adversely affect flowering and also increase the length of stem between leaf clusters.

Euphorbia Pulcherrima

POINSETTIA

This cheerful little plant has been developed from the large winter-flowering garden poinsettia as an indoor plant flowering in spring and summer. The true flowers are small and greenish-yellow but they are

surrounded by large leaf-like coloured bracts of red, pink or cream. These bracts only appear when nights are long, however commercial growers using darkened glasshouses and dwarfing chemicals can produce out-of-season short bushy plants covered with blooms. The coloured bracts usually last for at least two months. As it is not easy to flower the plants again, the whole bush should then be discarded or put into the garden.

LIGHT Bright but filtered.

TEMPERATURE As even as possible in normal conditions.

WATERING AND FEEDING
Water the soil thoroughly then wait for the first sign of a drooping leaf before watering again. Feeding is unnecessary.

SPECIAL CARE Avoid a draughty position.

COMMON PROBLEMS When buying, make sure the plant is free of insect pests.

Above ◆ **ECHEVERIA ELEGANS**
Left ◆ **EPISCIA**

Tree ivy will grow to about 1.5 m tall but at that height will need some support. Alternatively, it may be pruned into a bushy shape by cutting back the tips of the long stems in spring.

LIGHT Medium light but is tolerant of a wide range.

TEMPERATURE Normal room temperature. Cooler conditions in winter will induce a beneficial dormancy.

WATERING AND FEEDING While the tree ivy is growing, water thoroughly but allow the top of the soil to dry out before watering again. Reduce the amount in winter. Feed only when the plant is actively growing.

SPECIAL CARE Keep the leaves clean with a damp cloth and provide a humid atmosphere, especially in hotter conditions. Repot annually if the plant roots fill the pot.

COMMON PROBLEMS Premature leaf-drop in summer can be caused by overwatering. Watch for aphids, red spider mite and scale.

Above ◆ EUPHORBIA PULCHERRIMA
Left ◆ EUPHORBIA PULCHERRIMA 'ALBA' SP
Below ◆ FATSHEDERA X LIZEI

Fatshedera x Lizei

TREE IVY/ARALIA IVY/BOTANICAL WONDER/IRISH IVY

One of the easiest indoor plants to grow, this semi-climber is a botanical rarity; a hybrid with two quite different parents, aralia and ivy. It has inherited the hardiness of both but the large aralia leaves have been reduced to smaller but still glossy, dark green and five-lobed leaves, and the sprawling habit of an unsupported ivy has become upright.

Fatsia Japonica

ARALIA JAPONICA/JAPANESE FATSIA OR ARALIA

This fast-growing bushy shrub with its large, glossy, deeply lobed leaves has been a popular indoor plant for more than a century. In a large pot it may grow 1-1.5 m within two or three years, sometimes branching widely to become as wide as it is tall. Large globular clusters of small white flowers are followed by black berries annually on garden plants but seldom on indoor specimens.

LIGHT Bright filtered light.

TEMPERATURE Rather cool conditions are preferred during the growing period with even cooler ones, down to 5°C during the winter resting period.

WATERING AND FEEDING In spring and summer keep the soil thoroughly moist but as the weather cools restrict watering to allow the top of the soil to dry out before watering again. Use liquid or slow-release fertiliser during the growing season following the maker's instructions.

SPECIAL CARE The atmosphere should be kept humid if the temperature rises above 15°-18°C. Keep the leaves clean with a damp cloth and avoid leaf gloss preparations. Aralias may be pruned in spring if they are becoming too big. Repot annually using a heavy pot to balance the spreading plant.

COMMON PROBLEMS Watch for scale and mealy bug. Plants grown in warm rooms will become less resistant to disease.

Above ◆ **FATSIA (JAPANESE ARALIA)**
Right ◆ **FICUS ELASTICA**

Ficus

RUBBER PLANT

Members of this very large group differ widely, and even amongst the few grown indoors there are large and small leafed trees, shrubs and creepers. Although figs originate in the tropics and semi-tropics and all need a humid atmosphere, some will tolerate quite cool conditions. When growing in the ground fig trees may reach 15-30 m in height (a point to remember before planting out a rubber tree), but in containers they are seldom more than 2 m tall. Among the most well known is the weeping fig, *Ficus benjamina*, a graceful little tree with pendulous branches covered with small shining

pointed leaves, pale green when young, darkening as they mature; and the rubber plant, *F. elastica*, with its single upright stem and large, stiff, dark green oval leaves and its many cultivars, some with variegated foliage and others with less obvious differences. The fast-growing fiddle-leaf fig, *F. lyrata*, sometimes called *F. pandurata*, is another with a strong upright stem and large shining leaves waisted like a fiddle. The creeping fig, *F. pumila* (formerly *F. repens*), is a small prostrate or climbing plant with aerial roots and little, puckered green leaves. It can be used as ground cover or as a climber. The other form of creeping fig, *F. sagittata* (formerly *F. radicans*) is usually seen in its variegated form, *F.s.* 'Variegata'. The leaves are larger, up to 8 cm long, lance-shaped and grey-green with irregular creamy-white margins. It is not as hardy as *F. pumila*.

LIGHT Medium to bright light. To keep their coloured markings, variegated forms (with the exception of *F.s.* 'Variegata') need some direct sunlight but green leafed figs tolerate lower levels of light.

TEMPERATURE Normal warm room temperatures for most figs. The creeping fig will thrive in quite cold conditions and high temperatures may kill it.

WATERING AND FEEDING Water well then allow the top half of the soil to dry out before watering again. The creeping fig needs to be kept damp but not sodden at all times. Feed only in the growing season.

SPECIAL CARE Humid conditions keep plants healthy. Wipe the leaves with a damp cloth but avoid leaf-shine preparations. Cutting the top off the rubber plant or the fiddle-leaf fig will cause it to branch lower down but milky sap will flow from the wound. This may be sealed with a dusting of powdered charcoal. Repot in spring when the roots fill the pot. Figs like to be slightly cramped.

COMMON PROBLEMS Falling leaves may be the result of overwatering or a sudden change in temperature and humidity, however it is normal for old

leaves to fall. Watch for red spider if the atmosphere is dry. When rubber plants grow too big for the house they should be discarded. Their large and vigorous root systems can cause trouble in the average suburban garden.

Fittonia Verschaffeltii

NERVE PLANT/MOSAIC PLANT/PAINTED NET LEAF

The two forms of the nerve plant, *Fittonia verschaffeltii*, make attractive, low spreading plants with delicately patterned foliage. The oval leaves of the painted net leaf, *F. verschaffeltii*, are deep olive green with a network of rosy red veins while those of the mosaic or nerve plant, *F.v.* 'Argyroneura', are bright green criss-crossed with white veins. Small yellow flowers held in spikes of green bracts are sometimes produced but should be removed to encourage leaf growth.

LIGHT As these plants come from tropical jungle they need only medium light and no direct sunlight.

TEMPERATURE A warm even temperature about 18°C all year round.

WATERING AND FEEDING Water just enough to keep the soil moist and feed with weak liquid fertiliser during the growing season.

SPECIAL CARE High humidity is essential. Pinching back the tips of the long trailing stems will make a bushier plant. Repot in spring only if roots fill the pot.

COMMON PROBLEMS None.

Above ♦ **FITTONIA VERSCHAFFELTII**

Gasteria Verrucosa

WARTY OX TONGUE

This sturdy succulent has strap-shaped, fleshy, dark green foliage covered with small pearly warts. The leaves form a distinctive arrangement as they grow in two opposing ranks but young plants soon sucker to form a closely packed clump. The leaves are up to 15 cm long, and provided the warty ox tongue has a resting period during the cold weather it will produce 30 cm long flowering stems with small red and pink blooms in later spring or summer.

LIGHT Medium light, no direct sunlight.
TEMPERATURE Normal room temperatures from spring to autumn. Cooler conditions in winter will give the plant a resting period.
WATERING AND FEEDING Water enough to moisten the soil while the plant is growing but do not water again until the top of the soil is dry. Water less during the resting period but do not let the soil dry out. Provided the soil in the pot contains a little slow-release fertiliser, no further feeding should be necessary.
SPECIAL CARE Like most succulents the ox tongue prefers a dry atmosphere. When repotting in summer allow room in the new pot for the plant to spread as it may produce offsets.
COMMON PROBLEMS It is normal for the oldest leaves to die, but if younger ones brown they may have been burnt by direct sunlight. Overwatering will cause rotting.

Above ◆ **GASTERIA VERRUCOSA**

Gynura Sarmentosa

VELVET PLANT/PURPLE PASSION VINE

This trailing tropical plant has irregularly lobed leaves which, when young, are covered with thick purple down. As the leaves mature the down disappears and the green surface beneath shows through. Orange-yellow, daisy-like flowers are produced in spring and summer but since they have an unpleasant scent, they should be nipped in the bud so as to channel growth into the foliage. The long stems may be up to 1 m in length which makes the purple velvet plant look impressive in a hanging basket. There is some confusion over both the botanical and common names of this plant which may be a form of the similar *G. aurantiaca*.

LIGHT Bright with some direct sun except at the hottest times.
TEMPERATURE Normal room temperature about 18°-20°C.
WATERING AND FEEDING Allow the top 1-2 cm of soil to dry out between waterings during warm weather but reduce the amount given as the temperature

Above ◆ **GYNURA SARMENTOSA**

drops. Feed throughout the year but only monthly as lush growth becomes coarse and prone to disease.
SPECIAL CARE The velvet plant likes a humid atmosphere. Do not mist-spray as this may spot the leaves. Nip back long stems when they become lanky.
COMMON PROBLEMS Lack of purple down on young growth may be caused by too little light and by mites having distorted the young foliage.

Harpephyllum Caffrum

KAFFIR PLUM

The Kaffir plum, *Harpephyllum caffrum*, is an evergreen South African tree and is a familiar sight in frost-free parks and open spaces because it is easy to cultivate and has attractive, dark green, glossy foliage. While young it also makes a handsome indoor plant with large leaves, 30-35 cm long, composed of curved leaflets arranged along a central rib. The young leaves are dull red but change to dark green as they mature, and in autumn a few may turn scarlet. By the time it is 2-3 years old the Kaffir plum may have reached 1.5-2 m in height and be too large for the house. If planted in the garden it will make a broad-headed tree 10-12 m in height.

LIGHT Bright with some direct sunlight.

TEMPERATURE Normal warm room temperatures.

WATERING AND FEEDING Water thoroughly during the warm months but reduce the supply during the colder ones. Use a high nitrogen fertiliser, following the maker's instructions, from spring to early autumn.

SPECIAL CARE Wipe the leaves clean with a damp cloth or take outside and hose gently. Avoid leaf gloss preparations. It will probably not need repotting before it becomes too large for the house.

COMMON PROBLEMS A hardy trouble-free plant.

Haworthia Reinwardtii

This easily grown succulent usually forms a tidy column of neatly stacked leaves packed so closely that the stem, up to 15 cm long, is completely hidden. Each thick leaf is a dark green elongated triangle held almost erect so that only the underside, heavily spotted with small pearly warts, is visible. Since the plant is grown for its foliage most growers remove the thin stems of small white flowers which appear periodically. In the second year offsets, short shoots, are formed around the base of the plant.

LIGHT Medium light is preferred.

TEMPERATURE Normal room temperatures with a cooler resting period at about 10°-12°C in late winter.

WATERING AND FEEDING In warm weather water well but allow the top of the soil to dry out before watering again. During the rest period water more sparingly but do not let the soil dry right out.

A little slow-release fertiliser added to the soil at the start of the growing season is sufficient.

SPECIAL CARE Avoid direct sunlight which may shrivel the leaves and turn them reddish-bronze. Repot in spring when the plant and offsets almost fill the pot using a broad rather than deep container as Haworthia species are shallow-rooted.

COMMON PROBLEMS Rotting is probably the result of overwatering.

Below ◆ **HARPEPHYLLUM CAFFRUM**
Bottom ◆ **HAWORTHIA REINWARDTII**
Right ◆ **HEDERA**

Hedera

IVY

Most of the numerous varieties of ivy available can be divided into two groups; one composed of the variegated forms of the Canary Island ivy, *Hedera canariensis*, and the other much larger group comprising varieties of the English ivy, *H. helix*. Both are climbing plants if some support is provided. The Canary Island ivies take longer to produce the aerial roots by which ivies attach themselves to suitable supports and are also slower to branch out into a well furnished plant. The leaves of both groups are leathery with three to five lobes but those of the English ivy

group are generally smaller, and likely to be much more deeply lobed and pointed. The many variations are in different colour combinations of green with white, cream, grey, or gold and in some the leaves have frilled margins.

LIGHT Bright light and some direct sunlight to keep the plants bushy. Hot sun may burn the young growth of the variegated Canary island ivies.

TEMPERATURE An even temperature, preferably cool, although ivies will tolerate a fairly wide range of temperature especially if humidity is raised in hotter conditions.

WATERING AND FEEDING Water well while actively growing but allow the top of the soil to dry before watering again. In winter reduce the amount of water but do not let the soil dry out completely. Use liquid or slow-release fertiliser following the maker's directions during the growing period.

SPECIAL CARE Keep the leaves dust free with a damp cloth or if possible take the pot outside and hose the plant gently. Avoid leaf shine preparations. Canary Island ivies are not quite as hardy as English ivies and prefer a slightly warmer position. Repot in spring when the roots fill the container.

COMMON PROBLEMS Lanky, sparse growth may be caused by insufficient light. In dry atmosphere red spider mite may cause trouble. Watch for scale.

Howea

KENTIA PALM/SENTRY PALM/THATCH PALM/CURLY PALM

These palms are among the easiest plants to grow indoors as they are tolerant of poor potting mix, low light, cool temperatures and dry atmosphere. Wrongly placed with the Kentia genus when they were first discovered, they are still frequently known by that name. The Belmore sentry palm or curly palm, *Howea belmoreana*, and the Forster sentry or thatch palm, *H. forsteriana*, are both feather-type palms with long-stalked arching fronds rising from a very short

Above ◆ **HOWEA**
Right ◆ **HOYA BELLA**

trunk. Both are slow-growing, usually producing only 1-2 new fronds each year. After many years they may reach 2.5 m in height and in breadth, although the Forster sentry palm has a wider spread. The differences between them are slight: both produce pairs of dull green narrow leaflets; those of the Belmore sentry palm join the central rib of the frond at an acute angle, while those of the Forster palm are almost flat which gives the plant a more spreading shape.

LIGHT Wide range of intensity tolerated but no direct sunlight.

TEMPERATURE Normal room temperature.

WATERING AND FEEDING While actively growing, the soil should be kept moist but not sodden, in winter water only enough to keep the soil just damp.

SPECIAL CARE Wipe the leaves with a damp cloth but avoid leaf shine preparations. Repot in spring only when the roots fill the pot.

COMMON PROBLEMS Watch for scale and mealy bugs, particularly in the root system.

Hoya

WAX PLANT

Two species of wax plants are popular indoor plants, one a climber, the other a trailer. Both have fleshy leaves and clusters of thick, star-shaped flowers in summer. *Hoya bella* is a bushy plant with pendulous stems, making it well adapted to a hanging basket. The pale green, narrow, lance-shaped leaves are arranged in pairs along the stems and the starry, white flowers in small clusters have purplish-pink centres. *Hoya carnosa* has bigger, dark green, glossy oval leaves and drooping hemispherical clusters of perfumed pale pink flowers with red centres. The long stems, which have small aerial roots, may be trained up supports.

LIGHT Bright light including direct sunlight for several hours a day.

TEMPERATURE Normal room temperature.

WATERING AND FEEDING

While the plants are actively growing, water regularly but allow the top of the soil to dry between waterings. In the resting period water more sparingly. Use liquid or slow-release fertiliser during spring and summer only.

SPECIAL CARE Do not pick the flowers or remove the short thick stems which carry them as they will produce the following year's blooms. The wax plant prefers a well-ventilated, airy position but does not like draughts. Repot in spring when roots fill the pot.

COMMON PROBLEMS Lack of flowers may be caused by removal of flowering stems. On the other hand, the plant may be too young or there may not be enough light.

Hyacinthus

DUTCH HYACINTH

Spring-flowering bulbs with big heads of heavily scented blooms, hyacinths are usually available in late winter or spring when the flowers open. Colours range through white and several shades of cream, blue and pink and

Right ◆ **HYACINTHUS**
Below ◆ **HYACINTHUS ORIENTALIS**

occasionally orangy-red. If a hyacinth is bought just as the first flowers on the spike are opening it should last for several weeks, especially as many of the bulbs will produce a second smaller flower spike before the first is spent.

To grow your own hyacinths, buy the bulbs in autumn, choosing only those in which the circle of old roots is much smaller than the circumference of the bulb itself. The most suitable hyacinth vase would be a narrow necked container, transparent so the roots can be seen. Fill the vase with

water and add a small piece of charcoal to keep the water sweet. Sit the bulb in the neck, root side down and just above the water level. Shut the container in a dark cupboard until the thick white roots are well grown and the leaf shoot is 3-5 cm tall, then move it to a shady spot until the leaves have changed from yellow to green. When that happens, move it to a brighter area. Top up the water carefully as it is absorbed, but never let the bulb touch the water.

Both soil-potted and watergrown

hyacinths should be discarded after flowering unless they can be put in the garden as soon as the flowers are spent. If the climate is suitable, they will continue to produce small flower spikes each year.

LIGHT Bright and some cool direct sunlight.

TEMPERATURE A cool atmosphere prolongs the life of the blooms.

WATERING AND FEEDING Keep the soil just moist for potted hyacinths and keep the water level up to the roots for those growing in water. Before planting in the garden add some bulb food to the soil.

SPECIAL CARE Use a thin bamboo stake to support large flower heads.

COMMON PROBLEMS Only healthy bulbs will produce big blooms. Make sure the roots are well grown before bringing the bulbs out of the cupboard or the flower will not have a long stalk.

Hypocyrta

CLOG PLANT/MINIATURE POUCH FLOWER

These little shrubs with their small, closely set, glossy, dark green leaves would be attractive as indoor plants for their foliage alone. However the tiny flowers are even more striking and are produced in great numbers over a long period in summer. They have small pouched tubes with five small lobes, in shades of orange and red, deepening as they age. The clog plant, *Hypocyrta glabra*, makes a bushy plant about 20 cm high but much wider, while the miniature pouch flower, *H. nummularia*, has long trailing stems making it suitable for hanging baskets.

LIGHT Bright but no direct sunlight.

TEMPERATURE Normal warm room temperature from spring to autumn. In winter cooler conditions, not below 13°C, are necessary to ensure flowering the following summer.

Above ◆ **HYPOCYRTA RADICANS**
Below ◆ **HYPOESTES SANGUINOLENTA**

WATERING AND FEEDING
Keep the soil moist during the growing season but water more sparingly during the winter rest period. Feed with liquid or slow-release fertiliser only during the growing period, following the maker's instructions.
SPECIAL CARE These plants like a humid atmosphere, especially if temperatures rise. Flowers are carried on new spring growth, so prune in late winter to encourage new shoots.
COMMON PROBLEMS Lack of flowers may be the result of insufficient light or no proper resting period in winter.

Hypoestes Sanguinolenta

POLKA DOT PLANT/FRECKLE FACE/BABY'S TEARS/FLAMINGO PLANT

This branching, fast-growing little plant, best kept at about 50 cm or less, is grown for its unusual foliage. It is also known as *Hypoestes phyllostachya*. The pairs of ovate leaves, which have a gritty texture, are dark green heavily splashed with pink. When the small spikes of insignificant, lilac-coloured flowers appear in spring they should be cut off so that growth will be channelled into the foliage. Although cold conditions will kill the polka dot plant, cooler temperatures may only cause the stems to die down, in which case fresh shoots will appear in spring.
LIGHT Filtered bright light to keep the plant bushy. No direct sunlight.
TEMPERATURE Normal room temperature.
WATERING AND FEEDING
Water enough to keep the soil moist from spring to autumn but more sparingly in cold weather. Feed only during the growing season with liquid or slow-release fertiliser following maker's instructions.
SPECIAL CARE A humid atmosphere is needed for the polka dot plant or the

Above ♦ **KALANCHOE**

leaves may drop. Prune back long stems in spring and pinch back new growth to encourage bushiness.
COMMON PROBLEMS Small brownish-green leaves with poor markings are probably caused by leaving the plant in direct sunlight.

Kalanchoe Blossfeldiana cultivars

There are many forms of this easily grown small succulent which are admired for their brightly coloured flowers. In winter the clumps of closely packed, fleshy, dark green leaves produce a number of flowering stems about 30 cm tall, each topped with a spreading head of small flowers ranging in colour through yellow,

orange, red or pink. If they are bought in winter when they are coming into flower they should last for two to three months. When flowering finishes they are often discarded or put out into the garden but they may be kept in pots if they are pinched back to keep the plant compact. They will need short days, only ten hours of daylight, before they will flower again.
LIGHT Bright with direct winter sun.
TEMPERATURE Normal room temperature.
WATERING AND FEEDING
In warm weather while growing keep the soil just moist, allowing the top half to dry out before watering again. In winter water more sparingly. Feed only if the plants are kept after flowering.
SPECIAL CARE A dry atmosphere is preferred.
COMMON PROBLEMS Foliage turning red is a result of overexposure to the sun. Mildew is caused by high humidity.

Leea Coccinea 'Rubra'

An evergreen shrub grown in the garden in warm climates, *Leea coccinea* also makes a handsome foliage plant for indoors when young. In a container it may reach 0.5-1 m in height. The young leaves are deep plum red, unrolling rather like a fern frond to become deep bronze red when mature. Each leaf is large and composed of an uneven number of shining narrow leaflets with slightly ruffled margins. In the garden even young plants of the species produce small red flowers with flattened heads followed by red berries but these do not often appear on plants grown inside.
LIGHT Medium to bright but filtered.
TEMPERATURE Warm through most of the year. Cooler conditions in winter

encourage the plant to rest.

WATERING AND FEEDING
Keep the soil thoroughly moist during the growing season but allow the top half to dry out between waterings when the plant is resting. Feed in spring and summer.

SPECIAL CARE A humid atmosphere is preferred. Prune back in winter to encourage new growth.

COMMON PROBLEMS Leaf-drop in winter is quite normal.

Licuala Spinosa

FAN PALM/QUEENSLAND FAN PALM

One of a large group of fan palms, *Licuala spinosa* forms a distinctive cluster of stems as it ages. Each stem carries thorny, slender-stalked circular leaves divided into broad, radiating, wedge-shaped segments. The leaves' ribbed and pleated segments end abruptly as though cut off with large pinking shears, unlike those of the lady palm, *Rhapis excelsa*. Shining orange fruits borne by *L. spinosa* are rarely seen on indoor specimens.

LIGHT Bright but filtered; no direct sun.

WATERING AND FEEDING
Keep the soil thoroughly moist during the growing period and only slightly drier in winter. Use slow-release or liquid fertiliser in spring and summer only.

SPECIAL CARE A native of the tropics, this fan palm needs high humidity. Wipe the leaves clean with a damp cloth but avoid leaf gloss preparations.

COMMON PROBLEMS Watch for scale and mealy bug. Lack of humidity may cause the tips of the fronds to brown.

Below ◆ **LICUALA SPINOSA**

Liriope Muscari

BIG BLUE LILY-TURF

Although both the plain and variegated leaf forms of this grasslike plant are often grown in gardens, it is not common knowledge that they make good indoor plants as well. The long, narrow, dark green leaves form thick clumps and in late summer and autumn tall flower stems appear, up to 30 cm in height. The stems carry narrow, tightly packed heads of small lilac-coloured flowers. Some varieties of this species have striped white leaves or pale lilac or white flowers.

LIGHT Bright but filtered; no direct sunlight.

TEMPERATURE A wide range of temperatures is acceptable from spring to autumn. A cool resting period is needed in winter.

WATERING AND FEEDING
Water enough to thoroughly moisten the soil during the growing period but allow the top to dry out before watering again. In the resting period water more sparingly. Use liquid fertiliser during the growing period only, following the maker's instructions.

SPECIAL CARE Remove spent flower stems and old leaves.

COMMON PROBLEMS Lack of flowers is probably caused by insufficient light.

Livistona Australis

CABBAGE TREE PALM/AUSTRALIAN FAN PALM/CHINESE FAN PALM/FOUNTAIN PALM

This native palm was eagerly sought in Australia's early colonial days because the leaves could be woven into baskets or broad-brimmed hats and the terminal bud provided a succulent substitute for cabbage. Today the cabbage tree palm, *Livistona australis*, makes an attractive indoor potted plant. It has a number of circular leaves, pleated and divided into radiating segments falling vertically at the ends. The stalks have sharply toothed margins.

LIGHT Bright but filtered.

TEMPERATURE A native of the east coast from Queensland to eastern Victoria, the cabbage tree palm thrives in any normal room temperature down to 7°C.

WATERING AND FEEDING Water enough to moisten the soil thoroughly but allow the top to dry before watering again. If the temperature falls in winter water more sparingly, although in a heated room the plant will continue to grow, so keep up the supply of moisture. Feed in the growing season.

SPECIAL CARE Humid conditions are necessary, especially when the plant is young. Wipe leaves clean with a damp cloth but avoid leaf shine preparations. Repot when roots fill container, usually every two years.

COMMON PROBLEMS Watch for scale, mealy bug and leaf-rolling caterpillars. Brown tips to foliage may be caused by dry air or dry soil.

Mammillaria Bocasana

POWDER PUFF CACTUS

The *Mammillaria* group contains popular cacti of all shapes and sizes. Most are small, spiny plants, globular in shape, but some grow into cylinders as they mature. Some form clusters, others branch from the base. The spines are long and fine in some and woolly in others. Unlike most, these cacti are not ribbed but have protuberances or tubercles which carry the clusters of spines at their tips. The bell-shaped flowers appear in a ring at the top of the same stem that carried blooms the previous year. Brightly coloured seed

pods may follow after the flowers. While some *Mammillaria* species are extremely difficult to grow, the powder puff cactus, *M. bocasana*, is easily grown and rapidly forms a cushion of blue-green globular stems covered with clusters of fine, silky, white spines. Appearing in spring, the flowers are small and creamy.

LIGHT Direct sunlight. The container should be turned regularly to maintain an evenly shaped plant.

TEMPERATURE Normal room temperature during spring and summer when the plant is growing. A cool resting period in winter, down to 7°-10°C, is essential for good health and flowering.

WATERING AND FEEDING Water sparingly in spring and summer, allowing the top of the soil to dry out before watering again. During the resting period water only enough to prevent the soil drying out completely. Add slow-release fertiliser to the soil at the start of the growing season.

SPECIAL CARE A dry atmosphere is important. Water from below, being careful not to let water stand on any part of the plant.

COMMON PROBLEMS Poor growth will generally prevent the plant flowering the following year. Rotting may be caused by overwatering or standing in water.

Above ◆ **LIRIOPE MUSCARI**
Below ◆ **LIVISTONA AUSTRALIS**
Top Left ◆ **MAMMILLARIA BOCASANA**

Maranta Leuconeura

PRAYER PLANT

Prayer plants are grown for their strongly patterned foliage and are named for their curious habit of folding their leaves at night. They have smaller leaves than *Calathea, Ctenanthe* and *Stromanthe* but are otherwise similar and are often confused with them. The leaves are held horizontally during the day but at night move to a vertical position like hands held in prayer. Although the colours vary between the different forms, most prayer plants have green velvety leaves with clearly marked veins, sometimes in a paler green, sometimes bright red, with deeper green or dark brown blotches between the lateral veins. The undersides of the leaves are purplish-red. The flowers are insignificant. All *Maranta* varieties require similar conditions.

LIGHT Medium light; no direct sunlight.

TEMPERATURE An even warm temperature of 18°-21°C is preferred; never below 13°C.

WATERING AND FEEDING
Keep the soil moist during the growing season. When the plant is resting in winter, allow half the soil to dry out before watering again. Do not leave the plant standing in water as this will rot the roots. Use fertiliser during the growing season.

SPECIAL CARE Prayer plants come from tropical forests and need high humidity. Avoid mist spraying as the leaves are easily marked. Repot in spring using a wide, shallow container to accommodate the spreading shallow root system, and to allow the leaves to hang over the damp soil.

COMMON PROBLEMS Fading patterns may be caused by too much or too little light. Browning of leaf tips or margins may result from dry soil or dry atmosphere.

Monstera Deliciosa

FRUIT SALAD PLANT/SWISS CHEESE PLANT

When young the fruit salad plant, *Monstera deliciosa*, gives little indication of its future magnificent shape and size. The young long-stalked leaves, about 20 cm in length with perhaps a few small perforations, will eventually expand up to 60 cm in length and 45 cm across, the blades perforated and

Right ◆ **MARANTA**

Below ◆ **MONSTERA DELICIOSA**

the margins slashed with deep divisions. The thickened stem grows slowly but produces long heavy aerial roots which will cling to a suitable strong support. Given the right conditions it will grow to 4-5 m tall. The fruit, which is edible, is rarely produced on indoor plants.

LIGHT Bright, filtered light with some direct winter sunlight.

TEMPERATURE Normal room temperature with a minimum of 13°C in winter.

WATERING AND FEEDING Keep the soil moist in spring and summer but water more sparingly in winter. Never let the pot stand in water as the roots will rot. Feed only during spring and summer.

SPECIAL CARE Provide a humid atmosphere. Train the aerial roots on to the surface of the pot or round some strong, moisture-holding support but not on to the wall. Wipe the leaves clean with a damp cloth.

COMMON PROBLEMS Except on young plants, small unperforated leaves are probably the result of too little light.

Above ◆ **NEMATANTHUS**
Below ◆ **NEOREGELIA CAROLINAE**

Nematanthus Longipes

THREAD FLOWER

This little evergreen shrub has drooping fleshy red stalks along which are spaced shiny oval green leaves edged with red. It seldom grows to more than 45-50 cm in height. The red flowers with their pouched tubes are carried in orange calyces which persist long after the flowers have fallen. They appear in winter providing a bright contrast with the glossy foliage. Another of the species, *N. fluminensis*, has green leaves heavily marked with purple on the undersides and pale orange flowers.

LIGHT Good but filtered with some cool direct sunlight in winter.

TEMPERATURE Normal room temperature and a warm position in winter.

WATERING AND FEEDING Keep the soil just moist during spring and summer but be careful not to overwater as the roots are susceptible to rot. In winter water less without letting the soil dry out. Feed during the growing season using liquid or slow-release fertiliser and following the maker's directions.

SPECIAL CARE A humid atmosphere is necessary for good growth, especially during hot weather. In spring, as the plant begins to grow, repot when the roots fill the pot.

COMMON PROBLEMS Collapse of the plant may be caused by root rot.

Neoregelia Carolinae 'Tricolor'

BLUSHING BROMELIAD

This captivating member of the bromeliads makes an open rosette about 60-70 cm across composed of narrow, strap-shaped leaves boldly striped in cream and white with spiny margins. When about to flower, which can be at any time of the year, the youngest leaves flush with crimson. A central vase of short crimson-red bracts surrounds the cluster of small, inconspicuous violet and white flowers which are formed just above the level of the water held in the central vase. When flowering finishes, the whole rosette dies back leaving several small offsets around the base. These will take at least four years to reach flowering stage.

LIGHT Bright with some direct sunlight to maintain colour.

TEMPERATURE Normal room temperature preferably not below 16°C.

WATERING AND FEEDING Keep the central vase filled with water and the soil moist; allow the top third to dry out before watering again. Use weak liquid fertiliser for both the vase and the soil.

SPECIAL CARE Keep the atmosphere humid, particularly at flowering time. Change the water in the vase every 3-4 weeks.

COMMON PROBLEMS Fading colours may be caused by too little light.

Nephrolepis Exaltata cultivars

BOSTON FERN/ERECT SWORD FERN

The many varieties of *Nephrolepis exaltata* are often grouped together as Boston ferns as this was the first variety to gain popularity. The thickened creeping stems give rise to a large number of long narrow fronds, up to almost 1 m in length, divided into narrow segments. These may be divided again making them ruffled, curled or lacy for all or part of their length depending on the variety. Erect at first, the fronds arch out as they mature until they almost completely cover the container in which they are grown.

LIGHT Bright, no direct sunlight.

TEMPERATURE Normal room temperatures not less than 10°C.

WATERING AND FEEDING Keep the soil thoroughly moist all the year round as the Boston ferns will continue to grow in winter. Only if the temperature falls close to 10°C should the top of the soil be allowed to dry out between waterings. Use half-strength liquid fertiliser unless the manufacturer gives specific instructions for ferns.

SPECIAL CARE A humid atmosphere is preferred. Remove any fronds which revert to the plain sword fern. Repot in spring if the roots fill the container.

COMMON PROBLEMS Old fronds brown and die naturally. Watch for scale on the stems.

Nicodemia Diversifolia

INDOOR OAK

Recently introduced as an indoor plant the indoor oak, *Nicodemia diversifolia*, may be grown in a hanging basket but may also be trained as a small bushy shrub suitable for a pot. According to the most recent classification, it should now be called *Buddleia indica* but it is generally known under its old name. The mid-green leaves of this easily grown plant are similar in colour and shape to the round lobed leaves of the English oak although they are not shed in winter. Young foliage is often reddish.

LIGHT Bright including some direct sunlight.

TEMPERATURE Normal room temperatures. Cool temperatures down to 10°C in winter.

WATERING AND FEEDING Water well during warm weather allowing the top of the soil to dry before watering again. Water more sparingly in winter. Feed only in the growing period.

SPECIAL CARE There is no need to provide a humid atmosphere but if possible take the pot outside to gently hose off the dust. Pinch back new growth to maintain a bushy shrub. Repot in spring if the roots fill the container.

COMMON PROBLEMS The indoor oak is prone to attack by red spider in warm, dry weather. Mist-spraying will help to prevent this.

Left ◆ **NEPHROLEPIS EXALTATA**
Above ◆ **NICODEMIA DIVERSIFOLIA**

Notocactus

Although these hardy little cacti come from the hot grassy plains of South America, they grow there under the shelter of the scrub and so are accustomed to some shade. The golden ball cactus, *Notocactus apricus*, is a light green, ribbed, globular plant densely covered with yellowish-red spines. In spring quite young specimens will produce short-lived but magnificent yellow, funnel-shaped flowers around the top of the plant. There are a number of other *Notocactus* species, most of them globular and producing flowers in a shade of yellow. Almost all of them flower when very young.

LIGHT Bright but not too much hot direct sunlight.

TEMPERATURE Normal room temperatures. Will tolerate cooler conditions during the winter resting period.

WATERING AND FEEDING Water well during the warmer months but make sure the drainage is good. Reduce the watering in the resting period. Apply slow-release fertiliser at the start of the growing season.

SPECIAL CARE Any offsets appearing around the base may be removed and potted in sand, keeping the young plants in the shade until they begin to grow.

COMMON PROBLEMS Rotting caused by overwatering in cool periods.

Top ◆ **NOTOCACTUS APRICUS**
Above ◆ **OXALIS HEDYSAROIDES**

Oxalis Hedysaroides

CHINESE FIREFERN

To many Australian gardeners the thought of cultivating *Oxalis* species is almost unbelievable because some are troublesome weeds in several tropical countries. However, the Chinese firefern, *Oxalis hedysaroides*, is not a problem plant. It makes a shrubby upright bush not more than 20 cm in height with deep red leaves each composed of three egg-shaped leaflets, rather like a clover leaf. If the weather becomes cold and cloudy or if they are touched the leaves are inclined to droop downwards temporarily. The small, five-petalled flowers are bright yellow, contrasting strongly with the foliage. They appear only if the firefern receives some direct sunlight every day.

LIGHT Bright with direct sunlight.
TEMPERATURE Warm conditions for active growth in spring and summer but will tolerate temperature as low as 5°C when resting in winter.
WATERING AND FEEDING Water thoroughly when the firefern is in active growth then allow the top of the soil to dry before watering again. In cold conditions water more sparingly. Use liquid or slow-release fertiliser, following maker's directions, only when the plant is actively growing.
SPECIAL CARE Keep in a well-ventilated, but not draughty, humid atmosphere. Repot in late spring only if roots have filled the container.
COMMON PROBLEMS Premature leaf-fall may be caused by a sudden change to cooler or less well-lit conditions.

SPECIAL CARE In hot dry weather increase the humidity. Repot annually in spring.
COMMON PROBLEMS Failure to produce flowers may be the result of too little light during the previous season.

Below ◆ **PEDILANTHUS TITHYMALOIDES**
Bottom ◆ **PACHYSTACHYS LUTEA**

Pedilanthus Tithymaloides 'Variegatus'

ZIG-ZAG PLANT/DEVIL'S BACKBONE/JACOB'S LADDER

Popular as a glass-house plant around 150 years ago in Britain, the zig-zag plant is still grown for its unusual rather than beautiful appearance. This succulent little shrub reaches about 60 cm in height and has fleshy stems which grow in a zig-zag pattern, changing direction every 2-3 cm at each joint. The leaves are greyish-green tinged with red and bordered with irregular creamy-white margins. The

Pachystachys Lutea

GOLDEN CANDLES

An old favourite which has been reintroduced after many years of neglect, golden candles, *Pachystachys lutea*, is a small bushy shrub less than 50 cm in height. Rather like a plain green, heavily veined version of the zebra plant in appearance, golden candles produce long-lasting golden yellow spikes of bracts from which poke short-lived small white flowers, a few at a time throughout the summer. While not an easy indoor plant to cultivate, golden candles is not as demanding as the zebra plant.
LIGHT Good but not direct hot sunlight.
TEMPERATURE Normal room temperatures, preferably around 18°C with a minimum of 13°C in winter.
WATERING AND FEEDING Water thoroughly and allow the top of the soil to dry before watering again. Water more sparingly in winter. Use liquid or slow-release fertiliser, following maker's directions, when the plant is actively growing.

Left ♦ **PELLAEA ROTUNDIFOLIA**
Above ♦ **PELLIONIA**

stems, when broken, secrete a milky, irritant sap. Unfortunately the terminal clusters of scarlet flowers are rarely produced indoors, but if grown simply for its foliage, the zig-zag is an easy plant to cultivate.

LIGHT Bright, with some direct but not hot sunlight.

TEMPERATURE Warm atmosphere; not below 13°C.

WATERING AND FEEDING Through spring and summer water sparingly, allowing half the soil to dry out before watering again. As the temperature falls restrict the water even more. Feed only during months of active growth.

SPECIAL CARE The zig-zag plant needs a dry atmosphere and prefers to be slightly pot-bound. Repot in spring only if roots fill the container.

COMMON PROBLEMS Mildew may be caused by a humid atmosphere.

Pellaea Rotundifolia

BUTTON FERN

This rather slow-growing New Zealand fern, *Pellaea rotundifolia,* is easily recognised by the distinctive shape of its leaflets which are round on young plants and mature to an oval shape. Growing to about 30 cm in height and rather spreading in habit, it is well-suited to a hanging basket. The wiry, creeping stems give rise to dark, scaly-stalked fronds which, when young, are not rolled but folded like a shepherd's crook. The fronds are divided into small, rounded waxy leaflets set alternately along the midrib.

LIGHT Medium light with no direct sunlight.

TEMPERATURE Normal room conditions. The button fern will happily tolerate cool conditions down to 8°-10°C but not temperatures above 21°C.

WATERING AND FEEDING Water frequently in summer keeping the soil

moist. In cold conditions the soil should be dry on top between waterings. Fertilise whenever the plant is growing actively, which may be all the year.

SPECIAL CARE Button ferns do not need a humid atmosphere unless the temperature rises above 21°C, when they should be mist-sprayed. In their natural habitat they grow in the rock cracks where good drainage is assured so they should never have their roots in stagnant water. Repot only when the plant fills the pot.

COMMON PROBLEMS Watch for scale.

Pellionia

RAINBOW VINE/SATIN PELLIONIA

The two species of *Pellionia* commonly grown indoors are trailing or creeping plants grown for their handsome foliage and useful for hanging baskets or as ground cover. The stems will take root at any joint which touches the soil. *P. daveauana* has succulent reddish stems with flat, lance-shaped, dark green leaves which are generally broadly and irregularly striped with pale silvery green along the midrib. *P. pulchra* has purplish stems and the light or greyish-green leaves are heavily netted in dark brown or black along the veins. The lower surfaces are purple and grey. The flowers of both species are insignificant.

LIGHT Bright to heighten the coloured markings but no direct sunlight.

TEMPERATURE Normal room temperatures, preferably warm and not below 10°-12°C in winter.

WATERING AND FEEDING During warm weather keep the soil moist but not waterlogged as these plants rot easily. In cooler conditions water more sparingly. Use liquid or slow-release fertiliser, following maker's instructions, only when the plant is growing actively.

SPECIAL CARE These plants prefer a humid atmosphere. Repot in spring if necessary.

COMMON PROBLEMS Rotting is almost certainly caused by over watering.

Peperomia

There are over 1000 species in this very large genus, among them several popular indoor plants differing in appearance but all with fleshy leaves and stems. In most the spikes of massed tiny cream or white flowers are held well clear of the leaves, although some species do not flower indoors. However the flowers are not particularly attractive and *Peperomia* species are grown chiefly for their foliage. Amongst the most common is the watermelon peperomia, *Peperomia argyreia* (once known as *P. sandersii*), which is stemless with long-stalked leaves, up to 10 cm in length, forming a loose rosette less than 30 cm in height. The plant's red stalks join its thick shield-shaped leaves inside the margin. The point at which stalk and leaf meet forms the centre of the leaf pattern, and from it broad silver stripes radiate across the smooth, dark green surface following the curved margin of the leaf. The flower spikes are white and less than 10 cm tall.

P. caperata is another rosette-forming plant, a little smaller than the watermelon peperomia. The stalks are pink and the dark green heart-shaped

leaves, which are heavily crinkled, are no more than 4 cm long. A number of white flower spikes are produced in summer and autumn, held well above the foliage. There are several similar varieties including the aptly named 'Emerald Ripple' which has a smaller, more closely packed rosette.

P. magnoliifolia 'Variegata', sometimes confused with *P. obtusifolia* 'Variegata', is a more robust plant. The thick, upright red-spotted stems reach about 30 cm before they droop. The oval leaves are thick and waxy, mottled green and bordered with a wide irregular band of cream. This variety does not normally flower indoors.

Above ◆ **PEPEROMIA**
Top ◆ **PEPEROMIA CAPERATA**

P. scandens 'Variegata' (sometimes called *P. repens* 'Variegata') is a trailer with floppy pinkish stems which can be more than 1 m in length. The pointed, heart-shaped leaves are pale green with a wide margin of creamy white and are widely spaced along the stems. Flowers do not normally appear on indoor plants. This variety does not lose its variegations when grown in a medium light, unlike the others mentioned.

A recent cultivar *P.* 'Aussie Gold' has rounded, greeny-gold leaves with brownish-red veins. Unless kept in bright light, the gold tends to revert to green.

LIGHT Filtered bright but cool sunlight for variegated foliage forms.

TEMPERATURE Normal room temperatures; not below 13°C in winter.

WATERING AND FEEDING It is easy to overwater these plants. Even in summer allow the topsoil to dry before watering again and in cooler weather water more sparingly. Feed with weak fertiliser during warm weather only.

SPECIAL CARE High humidity in warm weather. Pinch out the tops of young growth of *P. magnoliifolia* to encourage bushy growth. Repot in spring; but remember Peperomia species have small root systems and do not require large pots.

COMMON PROBLEMS Rotting at the base is almost certainly caused by overwatering.

Philodendron

PHILODENDRON/TREE LOVER/PANDA PLANT/FIDDLE LEAF/RED LEAF

Popular as large indoor plants, Philodendrons come from tropical and sub-tropical America. Although they rarely flower indoors their glossy foliage, usually large and interestingly shaped, makes them well worth growing. Most philodendrons have distinctive juvenile and adult foliage. Because they are easy to hybridise and they originate from a wide range of natural habitats, there is sometimes confusion over their classification. Most have plain green leaves since those with variegations are generally too difficult for normal indoor cultivation but some have reddish bronze stems and foliage.

Philodendrons may be divided into two groups: the self-supporters, which form a sturdy stem, and the climbers. Among the latter, a sturdy climber is

Left ◆ **PHILODENDRON SCANDENS**
Below ◆ **PHILODENDRON 'ORCHID JUNGLE'**

the fiddle leaf philodendron, *P. bipennifolium* (also known as *P. panduriforme*), which may grow rapidly to 2 m or more in height. The shining, olive green leaves are 30-35 cm long. Those of mature plants are three-lobed, the base lobes extended and the central one waisted, while the leaf lobes of young plants are less clearly defined. Warmth and humidity are important, and too little light will result in small dull leaves.

The red leaf or blushing philodendron, *P. erubescens*, needs a strong support as it is a vigorous climber which puts out aerial roots at each joint. The arrow-shaped leaves, up to 25 cm long, are shining bronze green with reddish brown lower surfaces.

The heart-leaf philodendron, *P. scandens* (which may be known as *P. cordatum* or *P. oxycardium* as there is still some confusion over classification), is another rapid climber with aerial roots. Its glossy, pointed heart-shaped leaves are 10-15 cm long when the plant is young but twice as big when mature. It will tolerate a wide range of temperatures and poor light although the latter will result in more widely spaced and smaller leaves. It may be trained to grow up a support or to trail down.

Among the popular self-supporting philodendrons which develop strong stems is *P. bipinnatifidum* whose stem is crowned with large, long-stalked leaves. In a mature plant the stalks may be 10 cm or more in length and the dark green leaves, arrow-shaped in outline but deeply divided into narrow segments, may be equally as long and almost as wide. In a young plant the stem is much smaller, the leaves more rounded in shape and the margins merely notched. *P.* x 'Burgundy' is a slow-growing hybrid which may require a little support but it is not a climber. When young, the stem and long leaf stalks are red as are the new lance-shaped leaves but as these mature they change to deep olive green with red undersides

Another self-supporting philodendron

is *P. selloum* which has deeply divided leaves rather like *P. bipinnatifidum*. Fleshy aerial roots grow from the stem which is patterned with marks left by fallen leaves. The leaf stalks are very long, up to 60 cm, and the waxy, dark green leaves grow up to 40 cm in length. The leaves on young plants are almost undivided. This philodendron will tolerate fairly cold conditions.

LIGHT Bright, but not direct sunlight, will sustain the most attractive growth.

TEMPERATURE Normal room temperatures with a minimum of 13°C for best results.

WATERING AND FEEDING In warm weather water thoroughly but allow the soil to dry out on top before watering again. Water more sparingly in winter, only enough to prevent the soil from drying out altogether.

SPECIAL CARE Although philodendrons tolerate a dry atmosphere, their appearance and growth will improve in a humid atmosphere especially if temperatures are high. Where aerial roots appear they should either be trained down on to the soil or around a moisture-holding support such as a moss-covered pole or thick piece of bark. Keep the leaves clean with a damp cloth but avoid leaf gloss preparations. Repot in warm weather but only if roots fill the container. Philodendrons prefer small pots but these must be heavy enough to balance the weight and spread of the plant.

COMMON PROBLEMS Premature leaf-drop may be caused by sudden change of temperature or light intensity. Yellowing of leaves may be the result of overwatering.

Phoenix

CANARY ISLAND DATE/DATE PALM/MINIATURE DATE PALM

These hardy, slow-growing palms normally have solitary stems patterned with the remains of fallen leaves. The feather-type fronds, arching out from the crown, are divided into narrow

Above ◆ **PHOENIX ROEBELENII**

segments, dull, deep green in the Canary Island date palm, *Phoenix canariensis*, and the pygmy date palm, *P. roebelenii*, but greyish-green in the fruiting date, *P. dactylifera*. The lowest segments are modified into sharp spines or prickles.

Although all three species are grown ornamentally the Canary Island date and the fruiting date palm are strong and vigorous, eventually growing too big for indoor use. The pygmy date palm however, is much smaller and less vigorous, seldom more than 1 m in height with a spread of 1.25-1.50 m. It can spend its entire life in a container.

LIGHT Direct sunlight will not burn these palms but the pygmy date palm prefers filtered light.

TEMPERATURE Normal room temperature. In winter, cooler temperatures around 10°-13°C will ensure a resting period.

WATERING AND FEEDING Keep the soil thoroughly moist during the

Above ◆ **PILEA**

Right ◆ **PLECTRANTHUS AUSTRALIS**

growing period but water more sparingly when the palms are resting. Feed only during the growing period.

SPECIAL CARE Any suckering stems which appear at the base may be removed. Occasionally wipe both sides of fronds with a damp cloth. Repot when roots appear on the surface.

COMMON PROBLEMS White webbing at the tips of new fronds is normal. Watch for mealy bug and scale which can be troublesome.

Pilea

ALUMINIUM PLANT/ WATERMELON PILEA/ FRIENDSHIP PLANT

There are several species of these small, soft-foliaged plants, all of which require the same conditions for good growth. The aluminium plant, *Pilea cadierei* is easy to grow, and forms a rather upright bush best kept trimmed to around 30 cm in height to prevent the stems becoming leggy. The pairs of oval, dark green leaves grow up to 8 cm in length,

the surface heavily puckered and splashed with shining silver between the veins. The flowers are insignificant. Dwarf forms, such as *P.c.* 'Minima' are sometimes available. The artillery plant, *P. microphylla*, also called *P. muscosa*, has minute, rich green leaves giving it the look of a fern. In summer the tiny greenish-yellow flowers give off puffs of pollen if touched. It makes a dense upright clump to 25 cm in height. There is also a variegated form where the foliage is splashed with pink and white. Creeping Charlie, *P. nummularii-folia*, is a fast-growing, trailing plant with pale green, rounded wrinkled leaves only 1 cm or so across. It is ideal as a ground cover or for a hanging basket.

LIGHT Medium light, no direct sunlight.

TEMPERATURE Rather warm conditions.

WATERING AND FEEDING Overwatering and poor drainage may cause rotting. Allow the top half of the soil to dry out before watering again. Feed only in warm weather.

SPECIAL CARE These plants need humid conditions. As they have small, shallow root systems they seldom need repotting. When they lose their looks they are best replaced by cuttings which can easily be struck.

COMMON PROBLEMS Premature leaf-fall is probably caused by over-watering but may be due to a polluted atmosphere.

Plectranthus

SWEDISH IVY/CANDLE PLANT

The different species of Swedish ivy produce delicate heads of small tubular flowers in white or shades of lavender, but they are seldom grown for their floral display. Generally their flower-heads are removed so that growth will be channelled into their foliage. Most are creeping plants, although one species, *P. australis*, is erect and shrubby, reaching as high as 1 m. The pointed oval leaves with their scalloped margins are similar to those of the closely related *Coleus* but are plain dark green. *P. oertendahlii*, known also as the prostrate *Coleus* or candle plant, has long trailing stems which may be 50 cm in length. Roots grow from the joints wherever they touch the soil. The rounded, slightly furry leaves are dark bronze-green with silvery white veins on the upper surface and purple beneath.

LIGHT Bright.

TEMPERATURE Normal room temperatures with a winter minimum of 10°-12°C.

WATERING AND FEEDING During warm weather keep the soil thoroughly moist without being waterlogged. Water more sparingly in the resting period. Use liquid or slow-release fertiliser in spring and summer following the maker's directions.

SPECIAL CARE In hot, dry weather these plants need a humid atmosphere. Pinch back new shoots to encourage bushy growth. Repot only if the plant is in good condition, otherwise train the last few centimetres of the stems on to the soil and, when these have taken root, cut them off from the old plant. Start afresh with these rooted cuttings.

Polypodium Aureum 'Mandaianum'

HARE'S FOOT FERN

A large and beautiful fern from Central America and one of the best for use indoors provided there is room to accommodate the metre-long pendulous fronds. This fern gets its common name from the huge creeping stems, thickly covered in pale, hair-like scales which give the appearance of hares' paws. The light blue-green fronds, which may be up to 2 m long in a mature plant, are deeply cut into long narrow lobes with rippling margins.

LIGHT Medium; no direct sunlight.

TEMPERATURE Normal room temperatures.

WATERING AND FEEDING Keep the soil thoroughly moist unless the temperature drops below 13°C when water should be given more sparingly. Feed with liquid fertiliser, following maker's instructions, but use at half strength unless specific directions for ferns are given.

SPECIAL CARE If the temperature rises above 20C or so, increase the humidity. When repotting be sure to keep the creeping stems uncovered and allow ample room for them to grow along the surface. Repot in spring.

Above ◆ **POLYPODIUM AUREUM**
Below ◆ **POLYSCIAS BALFOURIANA**

COMMON PROBLEMS The appearance of small brown spots along the central veins on the lower surface is normal. They contain the spores or fern seeds.

Polyscias Balfouriana

When grown indoors this small tropical tree makes a bushy, much-branched shrub of about 1 m in height. The green stems are spotted with grey and in young plants the dark green, leathery leaves are almost circular with rounded teeth on the margin. As the plant matures the leaves change their shape, each one composed of three round leaflets with coarsely toothed margins and a slightly wrinkled surface. The most commonly available forms are *Polyscias balfouriana* 'Marginata' which has leaves unevenly bordered in pale cream and *P.b.* 'Pennockii' carrying olive green leaves in which the veins are marked in cream.

LIGHT Bright; no direct sunlight.

TEMPERATURE Warm conditions above 16°C even in winter.

WATERING AND FEEDING Water thoroughly but allow the top 1-2 cm to dry before watering again. Use liquid or slow-release fertiliser only during the warm months, following maker's instructions.

SPECIAL CARE Humid atmosphere is important especially during hot dry weather. Keep the leaves clean with a damp cloth but avoid leaf shine preparations.

COMMON PROBLEMS If the atmosphere is dry, red spider mite may attack.

Polystichum Proliferum

MOTHER SHIELD FERN

A mature plant of the mother shield fern, *Polystichum proliferum*, has a trunk-like stem covered with dark brown glossy scales and pendulous triangular fronds up to 1 m in length and 30 cm in width. Each frond is much divided and changes from pale to dark green as it matures. Like the mother spleenwort, the mother shield fern produces little plants from the buds on the tips of mature fronds. These take root when the aging frond arches over to touch the soil. Given a large container this fern builds up into a dense colony. Alternatively the plantlets may be detached when the roots have formed and planted into small pots.

LIGHT Will accept a wide range of light intensity including some direct sunlight.

TEMPERATURE Normal room temperature.

WATERING AND FEEDING Water thoroughly from spring to autumn but reduce the quantity in cooler weather. Use weak liquid fertiliser only during the warmer months.

Above ◆ **PORTULACARIA AFRA**
Left ◆ **POLYSTICHUM PROLIFERUM**

SPECIAL CARE These are hardy ferns which are at their best in cool conditions. If young plantlets are removed, repotting should not be necessary for some time.

COMMON PROBLEMS The small, raised light brown spots on the undersides of some fronds are the normal spore-cases of the fern.

Portulacaria Afra

JADE PLANT

A hardy succulent growing like a miniature tree, the jade plant is more correctly called *Crassula portulacaria* but is often seen under its old name, *Portulacaria afra*. The branches and short leaf stalks are red and the almost circular leaves, only 1-2 cm across, are pale glossy green. The rarely produced flowers are like little pale pink stars. It is extremely slow-growing but may reach 1 m in height after several years. Although it tolerates neglect it responds to a little attention.

LIGHT Bright, including direct sunlight.

TEMPERATURE Normal room temperatures with a cooler resting period in winter.

WATERING AND FEEDING In warm weather allow the top half of the soil to dry out between waterings. In cooler weather water sparingly without allowing the soil to dry out. Use a liquid fertiliser during spring and summer.

SPECIAL CARE The jade plant flourishes in a well-ventilated position. As it prefers a slightly pot-bound condition, repot only when the roots fill the container.

COMMON PROBLEMS Leaf-drop may be caused by poor ventilation.

Primula Obconica

This colourful flowering plant becomes available as it begins to bloom in midwinter, the flowers generally remaining until early summer. It has rounded, hairy leaves and the flowers, which may be white or various shades of pink, red, lilac or blue, are carried in a globular cluster on a tall stem well clear of the foliage. Five or six of these stems may develop as the plant matures.

LIGHT Reasonably bright with cool sunlight.

TEMPERATURE Normal unheated room temperatures.

WATERING AND FEEDING Keep moist and feed every three weeks or so with weak liquid fertiliser.

SPECIAL CARE Picking off dead flowers will encourage fresh ones. The fine hairs covering the plant's stems and leaves may irritate some skins.

COMMON PROBLEMS Colours in the flowers will fade in poor light.

Above Right ◆ **PRIMULA OBCONICA**

Right ◆ **PRIMULA X POLYANTHA**

Primula x Polyantha

POLYANTHUS

Once thought of solely as plants for the garden, polyanthus, *Primula x polyantha* (originally a hybrid), are now sold in pots for use indoors. They are available as they come into flower in midwinter and, given the correct conditions, will continue to bloom for several weeks. Polyanthus come in a great variety of colours including white, yellows, oranges, reds, pinks and blues, and the flowers may be held in a rounded cluster on a single upright stem or each one may have its own, much shorter stem. Very often the leaves are almost hidden by the masses of blooms. The plant's particular requirements are similar to those for *primula obconica*.

LIGHT Reasonably bright with cool sunlight.

TEMPERATURE Normal unheated room temperatures. Some growers like to put polyanthus outside in a sheltered spot each night.

WATERING AND FEEDING Keep moist and feed every three weeks or so with weak liquid fertiliser.

SPECIAL CARE Picking off dead flowers will encourage fresh ones.

COMMON PROBLEMS Colours in the flowers will fade in poor light.

Above ◆ **SILVER PTERIS FERN**
Right ◆ **PTERIS CRETICA ALBOLINEATA**

Pteris

CRETAN BRAKE/TABLE FERN/SWORD BRAKE

Several species and a number of cultivars of these graceful ferns are grown indoors. The fronds are close together on the creeping stems, forming erect clumps or crowns which arch out as the plant matures. The Cretan brake, *Pteris cretica*, grows to about 45 cm with dark green fronds, triangular in outline and divided into long narrow leaflets; one terminal and up to four pairs at right angles to the centre rib. In the cultivar *P.c.* 'Albolineata' each leaflet carries a broad cream stripe down the centre. The Australian brake, *P. tremula*, grows much more quickly making a larger plant 0.75-1.0 m in height. The large, pale green fronds are delicate and lacy, unlike those of the Cretan brake.

Rebutia

CROWN CACTUS

This group of small cacti come from the mountainous regions of South America. They grow into clusters of globular stems with vertical ribs carrying groups of spines. In spring a profusion of funnel-shaped flowers, which last for several days, is produced around the base of the plant and the colours range through yellow, orange, red, pink, mauve and white. There are many species of crown cacti but most are easily grown provided they have well-drained soil. Amongst the most attractive are *Rebutia albiflora* formed of tiny (1 cm) globes covered with soft white spines and bearing white flowers striped with pink, *R. rubriflora* which has orange-red flowers and *R. violaciflora*, a form of *R. minuscula*, with short reddish-yellow spines and bright 3 cm lilac-red blooms.

LIGHT Bright but sheltered from hot sun.

TEMPERATURE Normal room temperature with a cool resting period in winter.

WATERING AND FEEDING Water well in the warm months but be sure the drainage is good. In the resting period allow the top 1-2 cm of soil to dry before watering again. A little slow-release fertiliser applied at the start of the spring should be sufficient.

SPECIAL CARE Rotate pot to ensure symmetrical growth. If repotting use a shallow dish and porous potting soil.

COMMON PROBLEMS Should be trouble-free but poor drainage and or overwatering in cold weather can cause rotting.

Above ◆ **REBUTIA RUBRIFLORA**

LIGHT No direct sun but a bright light.

TEMPERATURE Normal room temperatures down to a minimum of 13°C in winter.

WATERING AND FEEDING Keep the soil thoroughly moist particularly in hot weather. Use weak liquid fertiliser or follow the maker's directions if specific instructions for ferns are given.

SPECIAL CARE When the weather is hot and dry provide a humid atmosphere. Remove old fronds, cutting away carefully to avoid injuring young ones. Repot in spring when roots fill the pot.

COMMON PROBLEMS It is normal for the margins of fertile fronds to curl under as they are protecting the sporecases.

Rhapis Excelsa

LADY PALM/JAPANESE HAND PALM/BAMBOO PALM

One of the most prized indoor palms is the slow-growing lady palm, *Rhapis excelsa.* They grow in clumps formed as suckers arise around the base of the stem which is covered with a mat of fine dark fibres. The fan-shaped leaves, up to 50 cm across on old plants, are carried on slender stalks and divided into a number of radiating, ribbed and pleated segments which contract towards the blunt tip. Although mature specimens may reach the ceiling, those generally available are more likely to be 0.5-1 m in height. The lady palm may produce a spray of pink flowers.

LIGHT Bright but filtered.

TEMPERATURE Normal room temperatures, cooler in winter.

WATERING AND FEEDING Keep the soil thoroughly moist without allowing it to become waterlogged. If temperature is really cold water a little more sparingly. Feed only when the plant is actively growing.

SPECIAL CARE Provide a humid atmosphere, especially when the weather is hot and dry. Wipe the fronds clean with a damp cloth but avoid leaf shine preparations. As the palm is so slow-growing it will probably not need repotting for two or three years. If it is necessary it should be done as temperatures start to rise.

COMMON PROBLEMS Poor condition may be the result of draughts, hot direct sun, or inadequate or irregular watering. Watch for scale and mealy bug.

Rhipsalidopsis

Rhipsalidopsis is one of three Brazilian jungle cacti genera; the others being *Schlumbergera* and *Zygocactus*, which are often called, crab, claw or lobster cacti. This genus formerly included only one species, *Rhipsalidopsis rosea*, but now *R. gaertneri* has been transferred to it from *Schlumbergera* and there are also several hybrids. The stems are erect at first but droop as they age. They look rather like leaves with their flattened segments with notched edges although the oldest ones may be thickened and angular. The bristles are not hard, sharp or hooked, which makes the plants much easier to handle than other cacti. In early spring the funnel-shaped flowers appear at the ends of the stems. They may be solitary or in small clusters and the colours range throughout several shades of pink and red. See also the entries on *Schlumbergera* and *Zygocactus*.

Top Left ◆ **RHAPSIS EXCELSA**

Left ◆ **RHIPSALIDOPSIS**

LIGHT Medium with cool winter sunlight only. Short days and long nights are needed to initiate flowering so plants must be kept in unlit rooms in autumn and early winter.

TEMPERATURE Normal room temperatures not below 8°-10°C in winter.

WATERING AND FEEDING Keep the soil thoroughly moist in spring and summer then water more sparingly, allowing the soil to dry on top before watering again when the flower buds appear. Use liquid fertiliser following the maker's instructions in spring and summer or use a slow-release fertiliser at half strength.

SPECIAL CARE Plants will appreciate a spell outside in summer if they can be put in a shaded position. They also like to be mist-sprayed with room-temperature water in hot dry weather. Repot in early summer after flowering if roots fill the pot. Some growers believe too much root activity reduces flowering.

COMMON PROBLEMS Stunted plants with numerous short branches may be caused by high nitrogen fertiliser.

Rhoeo Spathacea

BOAT LILY/MOSES IN A CRADLE/THREE-MEN-IN-A-BOAT

A native of Mexico, the boat lily, *Rhoeo spathacea* (sometimes labelled *R. discolor*) is distinguished by a rosette of rather stiff leaves whose undersides are a vivid purplish-red which makes an interesting contrast with the green upper surface. The leaves grow up to 30 cm long and as the plant matures, the lower ones fall leaving a bare upright stem. For this reason boat lilies are suited to group planting where the bare stems may be hidden and the leaves make a good contrast to other foliage. The tiny, short-lived white flowers are enclosed by two purple, boat-shaped bracts which remain after the flowers have died. They are produced in summer low down among

Rhoicissus Capensis

CAPE GRAPE/EVERGREEN GRAPE VINE

The Cape grape or evergreen grape vine is a vigorous plant forming underground tubers and climbing by means of tendrils or, if no support is available, trailing over the edge of its container. Unlike the grape ivy, *Cissus rhombifolia*, often wrongly called *Rhoicissus rhomboidea*, the easily grown Cape grape has undivided, round or kidney-shaped leaves up to 20 cm across. Young foliage is covered with soft brown hairs which are retained on the undersides of mature leaves, the upper surface developing a glossy metallic green. The margins are coarsely wavy.

LIGHT Bright but no direct sunlight.

TEMPERATURE The Cape grape is an undemanding plant and will tolerate a wide range of temperature.

WATERING AND FEEDING Keep the soil thoroughly moist from spring to autumn but water more sparingly in winter, allowing the top of the soil to dry between waterings. Use liquid or slow-release fertiliser, following the maker's instructions in spring and summer only.

the leaves. There is an attractive variegated form *R.s.* 'Variegata' with yellow and white stripes on the green leaves.

LIGHT Bright but no direct sunlight.

TEMPERATURE Normal room temperatures but not below 10°-12°C.

WATERING AND FEEDING Keep the soil moist in warm weather when the plant is actively growing. Water more sparingly in cool weather, allowing the top of the soil to dry between waterings. Use liquid or slow-release fertiliser following maker's instructions, only in spring and summer.

SPECIAL CARE Keep the humidity high in warm weather. Unless lit from all sides rotate the container daily so that the plant remains upright. Repot annually in spring.

COMMON PROBLEMS The leaves' colour will be poor if there is insufficient light.

Top ◆ **RHOEO**

Above ◆ **RHOEO SPATHACEA**

Top Right ◆ **RHOICISSUS TOMENTOSA**

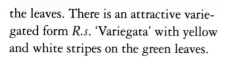

SPECIAL CARE In hot dry weather increase the humidity. Pinch back shoots to encourage bushy growth. Provide a firm support if a climbing plant is desired. Assist young plants by tying them to the support until they hold themselves. Plants which grow too big may be cut back in ate winter.

COMMON PROBLEMS This is usually a trouble-free plant.

Ruellia Makoyana

MONKEY PLANT/TRAILING VELVET PLANT

This warmth-loving, low, spreading plant looks best in a hanging basket. The branching stems may be 60 cm in length and carry pairs of ovate leaves about 8 cm long, olive-green on top, heavily marked with silvery-white along the veins, and deep violet below. Rosy-carmine, trumpet-shaped flowers up to 5 cm long, with five flaring rounded lobes, are freely produced in winter from the axils of the leaves.

LIGHT Bright but no direct sunlight.

TEMPERATURE As natives of Brazil, monkey plants need warm conditions not less than 13°C even in winter.

WATERING AND FEEDING After flowering finishes, water only enough to prevent the soil from drying out completely. From mid-spring water more abundantly but allow the top of soil to dry before watering again. During the growing season use liquid or slow-release fertiliser, following the maker's instructions.

SPECIAL CARE A humid atmosphere is essential for healthy growth. Repot at the end of the resting period only if the plant fills the pot.

COMMON PROBLEMS These plants are prone to attack by aphids.

Saintpaulia

AFRICAN VIOLET

These charming little plants are the delight of some growers but the despair of others. However, they are not difficult to maintain and bring into flower provided the correct conditions can be provided. African violets gained their common name not because they are botanically related to violets but

Top & Top Right ♦ **SAINTPAULIA**
Above ♦ **RUELLIA MAKOYANA**

because of the general similarity in the flowers and leaves. At one time the many hybrids available were all rosette-forming plants, 7-15 cm tall and about 30 cm across with velvety textured rounded leaves, pale or dark green on top and often reddish below, on long fleshy stalks. The single or double flowers were white or in shades of pink, red or purple with a prominent yellow pollen sac in the centre. Today miniature types with rosettes less than 15 cm across are available and there are plants with long trailing stems suitable for hanging baskets. The flowers may be produced at any time of the year and their petals may be bi-coloured or have heavily frilled margins. Single flowers will drop spontaneously but doubles will remain on the stalks after dying. Among the most easily grown hybrids are the 'Ballet' and 'Rhapsodie' or 'Melodie' strains.

LIGHT The ideal position would be in a bow window facing south-east, the glass screened with a light, transparent curtain. If there is insufficient light the leaf stalks will elongate and the central leaves become erect. If the light is too strong the plant will be stocky and the leaves a faded dull green. In either case few new flower buds will be produced.

TEMPERATURE African violets prefer 24°C by day and no lower than 20°C at night but will accept a range of 15°-26°C.

WATERING AND FEEDING
Water either by putting the pot in a deep container of water until the moisture has been drawn up to the top of the soil, or water from above, being careful not to wet the leaves. Use tepid water. Once the soil is thoroughly moist no more water should be given until the top centimetre or so of the soil is dry. In cooler temperatures less water will be needed. Fish emulsion is recommended by some specialist growers otherwise use a complete fertiliser with equal amounts of nitrogen, phosphate and potash. Use quarter-strength liquid fertiliser each time the plant is watered, or use slow-release fertiliser following the maker's instructions.

SPECIAL CARE High humidity is important for healthy growth. No draughts, but good ventilation will help to prevent fungal infection. Cut off dead flowers with a pair of scissors. African violets prefer a lightly pot-bound state and are happy in a container one-third of the diameter of the rosette of leaves. Repot at any time in warm conditions.

COMMON PROBLEMS Prone to attack by cyclamen mite. Rotting at the base is probably caused by overwatering. Watch for mildew and for mealy bugs on the foliage and in the soil.

Sansevieria

MOTHER-IN-LAW'S TONGUE/SNAKE PLANT/DEVIL'S TONGUE/BOWSTRING HEMP

Popular and resilient indoor plants, the various forms of mother-in-law's tongue, *Sansevieria*, tolerate considerable neglect and usually succumb only to overwatering or very cold conditions. The creeping underground stems of *S. trifasciata* 'Laurentii' give rise to narrow, upright leaves 35-45 cm tall, dark mottled green with wide creamy yellow borders. There are a number of other

varieties of mother-in-law's tongue, some with silver or gold variegations and some with much shorter leaves making squat rosettes. *S. zeylanica*, which grows up to 75 cm, makes an open rosette of greenish-grey leaves folded down the centre and horizontally banded with darker green. All forms of mother-in-law's tongue require the same general conditions.

LIGHT Medium to bright, including direct sunlight.

TEMPERATURE Normal room temperatures, preferably warm and not below 12°-13°C.

WATERING AND FEEDING
While the plant is actively growing, water enough to moisten the soil but allow the top to dry between waterings. In cooler weather water only enough to prevent the soil drying out altogether. Feed with a little slow-release fertiliser at the start of the growing period or use weak liquid fertiliser at no more than monthly intervals.

SPECIAL CARE Although these plants tolerate medium light they need brighter conditions for good growth but should not be moved suddenly into strong direct sunlight. Repot only when the plant fills the pot, probably after several years, as it prefers to be pot-bound.

COMMON PROBLEMS Rotting at the base of the leaves is almost certainly caused by overwatering in cold weather. Brown marks on the leaves are probably burns from sudden exposure to sunlight.

Right ◆ **SANSEVIERIA**
Far Right ◆ **SAXIFRAGA STOLONIFERA**

Saxifraga Stolonifera

MOTHER OF THOUSANDS/ STRAWBERRY GERANIUM

Often known as *Saxifraga sarmentosa*, the mother of thousands, *S. stolonifera*, is distinguished for its ability to produce numerous plantlets at the tips of long thin runners. It forms open tufts of circular olive-green leaves no more than 20-25 cm tall, patterned on top by white veins and covered with fine raised pink spots beneath. The leaves and the long pink stalks are covered with short stiff hairs. In summer small white flowers on long spikes appear. A variegated form *S.s.* 'Tricolor' has red, white and green foliage.

LIGHT Bright with cool direct sunlight.

TEMPERATURE Cool conditions with a minimum of 4°C in winter. The 'Tricolor' prefers slightly warmer conditions.

WATERING AND FEEDING From spring to autumn keep the soil thoroughly moist but water more sparingly in winter without letting the soil dry out completely. Feed only during spring and summer using liquid or slow-release fertiliser following maker's directions.

SPECIAL CARE If temperatures rise above 18°-20°C the plants may need added humidity. The variegated form needs more light to keep its colours. Plantlets may be detached and grown on. Repot in spring.

COMMON PROBLEMS Fairly disease-free but watch for mealy bug and scale.

Above ◆ SCHEFFLERA ACTINOPHYLLA
Right ◆ SCHEFFLERA ACTINOPHYLLA

Schefflera

UMBRELLA TREE

The Queensland umbrella tree, *Schefflera actinophylla*, perhaps better known under its old name, *Brassaia*, has long been grown in gardens and indoors in large containers. A more recent member of this genus is the much smaller dwarf umbrella plant, *S. aboricola*. It has the same glossy green leaves with radiating leaflets and long green stalks but is a much more compact plant with pliant branching stems. Another species, *S. venulosa*, once known as *Heptapleurum venulosum*, develops several main stems to form a small bushy plant which can be kept in a container for a long period. It tolerates cool conditions. Neither shrub is likely to flower indoors.

LIGHT Bright; no direct sunlight.

TEMPERATURE Normal room temperatures, not below 12°C in winter.

WATERING AND FEEDING Water thoroughly in spring and summer, allowing the top centimetre or so of soil to dry between waterings. Water much more sparingly as the temperature falls. Feed with liquid or slow-release fertiliser, following

maker's directions, in spring and summer only.

SPECIAL CARE Clean the leaves with a damp cloth but avoid leaf gloss preparations. When temperatures rise umbrella plants need a humid atmosphere. Repot annually in spring. Keep in a well-ventilated but draught-free position.

COMMON PROBLEMS Premature leaf-fall may be caused by low temperature, too much or too little water.

Schlumbergera

EASTER CACTUS/CLAW CACTUS

A popular trailing plant in many parts of the world, the *Schlumbergera* cactus is another native Brazilian cactus similar to *Rhipsalidopsis* and *Zygocactus*. Generally the cultivars and not the species of this genus are offered for sale. The stems are composed of flattened segments which are toothed or notched along the margins with a raised midrib. The oldest segments are likely to be rounded and woody. The arching, pendent stems make the plant particularly suited to hanging baskets. These plants flower in September and October which is equivalent in climate to March or April in the northern hemisphere where they found the name Easter cactus. The flowers are bright reds and pinks, their appearance elongated by their coloured basal bracts. They appear at the stem tips singly or in pairs and tend to close at night. See *Zygocactus* for new cultivars.

LIGHT Medium with cool winter sunlight only. Short days and long nights are needed to initiate flowering, so plants must be kept in unlit rooms in autumn and early winter.

TEMPERATURE Normal room temperatures.

WATERING AND FEEDING Although they recover fully if left unwatered for a while these cacti prefer well-watered soil most of the year. Some growers believe

that withholding water in late summer and early autumn until the plant begins to wilt will encourage more buds. Use a medium to low nitrogen liquid fertiliser or half-strength slow-release fertiliser while watering thoroughly.

SPECIAL CARE Rotate the pot so the plant will develop evenly. Repot after flowering finishes.

COMMON PROBLEMS Falling buds may be the result of a sudden change in temperature or a draught.

Scindapsus Aureus

DEVIL'S IVY/GOLDEN HUNTER'S ROBE

The devil's ivy is a popular indoor climber which, given good conditions, may reach 1.5-2 m in length indoors. Aerial roots will help to support the long stems if they are trained up a bark pole. The glossy, heart-shaped leaves of young plants, 10 cm or more in length, are bright green and irregularly splashed with

golden-cream. As the plant matures they become much larger and in old specimens may reach 30-60 cm, eventually becoming lobed and divided. The devil's ivy was formerly named *Pothos aureus* and has recently been changed to *Epiprenum aureum*. There are several varieties differing only in their leaf variegations and also another species, *S. pictus* 'Argyraeus', whose smaller leaves are blue-green with silver mottling and narrow silver margins. It is less easily grown needing slightly warmer conditions than devil's ivy.

LIGHT Bright but filtered.

TEMPERATURE A warm position all the year.

WATERING AND FEEDING During the growing period keep the soil moist but wait until the top dries before rewatering. Feed with liquid or slow-release fertiliser, following maker's directions, through spring and summer.

SPECIAL CARE A humid atmosphere is important. When in a hanging basket prune back the long trailers if they become straggly. Repot annually in spring.

COMMON PROBLEMS Fading leaf pattern is caused by too little light.

Sedum

STONE CROP/DONKEY'S TAIL

A group of hundreds of species of succulents ranging from small bushy plants to elongated trailing ones, these plants are generally grown for their decorative foliage, as flowers rarely appear on indoor specimens. Several of the more popular species are listed below.

Sedum adolphi makes a loose bush with erect or sprawling branches up to 20 cm long. The thick, fleshy, yellowish-green leaves with rounded points and fine red margins are packed closely along the stems. Round clusters of starry white flowers may be produced in spring.

Below ◆ **SCHLUMBERGERA GAERTNERI**
Right ◆ **SCINDAPSUS AUREUS**

S. *morganianum*, donkey's tail, has become very popular for hanging baskets in the last few years. The numerous drooping stems, up to 1 m in length, are closely packed with precisely arranged grey, cylindrical leaves giving the effect of circular plaiting. If produced, flowers are soft pink, appearing in spring.

S. *rubrotinctum*, jelly beans, is another familiar succulent whose thin, branching stems, upright at first, gradually bend down and take root where they touch the soil. The fat little cylindrical leaves are clustered near the tips. They are green in cool damp conditions but turn red, resembling jelly beans, when conditions are hot and dry. The slender stalks break off easily and will form roots where they fall.

S. *sieboldii* is also pendulous, with trailing red stems up to 20 cm or so in length, carrying fan-shaped, pink edged, grey-green leaves arranged in threes. Clustered heads of starry pink flowers may be produced on the tips of the stems in autumn. A variegated form produces leaves splashed with creamy yellow in the centre.

LIGHT As much direct sunlight as possible.

TEMPERATURE Normal room temperatures with cool conditions, 5°-10°C, in winter to ensure a resting period.

WATERING AND FEEDING
From spring to autumn water thoroughly but

Top Left ◆ **SEDUM MORANENSE**
Above ◆ **SELAGINELLA**

allow the top centimetre or so to dry before watering again. In cooler weather water more sparingly. A little slow-release fertiliser added to the soil at the start of the growing season is sufficient.

SPECIAL CARE Give sedums a well ventilated but not draughty position. Clean the leaves of dust by spraying gently. When repotting, in spring, use shallow wide containers to allow the plants to spread.

COMMON PROBLEMS Spindly elongated growth and poor colour will result from insufficient light. Any rotting at the base is almost certainly caused by overwatering.

Selaginella

MOSS FERN/SWEAT PLANT

Closely related to ferns, *Selaginella* also has some mossy characteristics. There are long wiry creeping stems both above and below ground, and thread-like roots, produced from the leaves, enable the plant to scramble easily over the ground making mossy mounds or trailing over the edge of the container. The tiny leaves, closely arranged on the stems, add to the plant's fern-like or mossy appearance. The trailing selaginella, *S. kraussiana*, quickly covers its pot forming a thick mat of bright green leaves and long stems, up to 30 cm in length. A golden leafed form, *S. martensii*, is a more upright plant although the stems, supported at first by the fine roots, arch over after they reach 10-15 cm. There are two forms with silvery variegations.

LIGHT Medium shade.

TEMPERATURE Normal room temperatures preferably above 10°C, but lower may be tolerated.

WATERING AND FEEDING
Keep the soil thoroughly moist but not waterlogged. Use only very weak fertiliser through spring and summer.

SPECIAL CARE Humid atmosphere is essential, as dry air will desiccate the foliage. Clipping back around the sides will control the spread if needed. Repot in spring into a wide, shallow container.

Sempervivum

HOUSELEEK/HEN AND CHICKENS

These succulents are a good choice if an easily grown small plant is wanted for a sunny window sill. The thick, fleshy triangular leaves form compact symmetrical rosettes and young ones are readily produced around the central one. If flowers are produced they are

Left ◆ **SEMPERVIVUM ARACHNOIDEUM**
Above ◆ **SENECIO CRUENTUS**

Senecio Cruentus hybrids

CINERARIA

Like the slipper flowers and chrysanthemums these brightly coloured little plants are not permanent indoor plants but can be bought as they come into flower in late winter or early spring. They bring a little of the gaiety of a spring garden into the house and are longer-lasting and less expensive than cut flowers. They are hybrids resulting from many years of breeding experiments, and as such are commonly known as the florist's cineraria. The daisy-like flowers are grouped into dome-shaped heads, 20-25 cm across, and the colours include white and shades of red, blue and purple, sometimes with a white ring. To enjoy them in the house as long as possible they should be given suitable conditions.

LIGHT Bright but not direct sunlight.

TEMPERATURE A cool room will lengthen the life of the flowers.

WATERING AND FEEDING Keep the soil moist; feeding is unnecessary.

SPECIAL CARE A humid atmosphere will help to prolong the life of the flowers.

COMMON PROBLEMS Before buying, inspect the plant for aphids.

carried on erect stems. When they die so also do the rosettes from which they emerged. The cobweb houseleek, *Sempervivum arachnoideum*, makes small rosettes about 5 cm across and the tips of the leaves are connected by many fine cobweb-like hairs. The houseleek or hen and chickens, *S. tectorum*, has smooth green leaves with reddish tips although there are other forms and hybrids with slightly different colours. The flowers, purplish-red on 20-30 cm stems, may be produced in summer.

LIGHT Bright with some direct but not too strong sunlight.

TEMPERATURE Alpine in origin, these succulents survive at normal room temperatures and prefer cool conditions down to 3°C.

WATERING AND FEEDING Water sparingly allowing the top centimetre or so to dry before watering again. In winter, water only enough to prevent the soil from drying out completely. A little slow-release fertiliser added in spring is sufficient.

SPECIAL CARE These plants like fresh air but not draughts. They are more resistant to drought than to overwatering so need well-drained soil. Repot in spring when plant covers container.

COMMON PROBLEMS Trouble free provided they are not overwatered which causes rotting.

Senecio Rowleyanus

STRING OF BEADS

A mat-forming succulent with long, flexible stems which take root as they spread across the soil. The little globular green leaves with pointed tips are strung unevenly along the stems, forming a dense mat if horizontal or a curtain if they are allowed to trail downwards. One plant will cover an area 60-90 cm in diameter. In autumn, small daisy-like flowers with a sweet perfume may be produced. Another species, *S. citriformis*, has leaves the shape of tiny lemons.

LIGHT Bright but only cool, direct sunlight.

TEMPERATURE Normal room temperatures with a winter minimum of 10°C to ensure a rest period.

WATERING AND FEEDING Water thoroughly in spring and summer but much more sparingly in cool weather, without letting the soil dry right out. Use either liquid or slow-release fertiliser in the warmer months, following the manufacturer's instructions.

SPECIAL CARE In hot dry weather mist-spray to raise the humidity. Repot in spring if plant fills the pot.

COMMON PROBLEMS Trouble free if not overwatered in cool weather when the plant should be resting.

Setcreasea Purpurea

PURPLE HEART

This sprawling, richly purple plant is untidy but among the easiest indoor plants to grow. The purple heart, *Setcreasea purpurea*, has bright violet coloured leaves up to 10 cm in length. The base of each is wrapped around the thick, violet coloured stem, and both

stems and leaves have a sparse covering of fine pale hairs. The stems are erect at first but when they reach 30-35 cm, bend over and become prostrate making the plant good for hanging baskets. Clusters of short-lived lilac-pink flowers appear between two spreading violet bracts at the tips of the branches in summer.

LIGHT Bright with direct sunlight except at the hottest times.

TEMPERATURE Preferably warm room temperatures for best growth but the purple heart will tolerate quite cool surroundings.

WATERING AND FEEDING Keep the soil thoroughly moist but not waterlogged in spring and summer. Water more sparingly as temperatures drop. Use liquid or slow-release fertiliser following maker's directions in spring and summer but avoid overfeeding as this will reduce the foliage colour.

SPECIAL CARE Prune back the tips of flowering shoots when flowers are spent to encourage new growth lower down the stems. Repot when plants fill the container, preferably in warm weather.

COMMON PROBLEMS Foliage losing its purple colouring is probably caused by insufficient light. Rotting results from overwatering especially in cool weather.

Below ◆ **SENECIO ROWLEYANUS**
Bottom Right ◆ **SETCREASEA PURPUREA**
Right ◆ **SINNINGIA SPECIOSA FYFIANA 'DEFIANCE'**

Sinningia Speciosa

GLOXINIA

With their richly coloured flowers rising from a circle of velvety green leaves, the many varieties of gloxinia, developed from *Sinningia speciosa*, generally begin to appear in nurseries in late Spring. The softly hairy leaves may be as much as 20 cm in length, their long stalks rising from the fibrous-rooted tuber. Large bell-shaped flowers with flaring lobes bloom in a multitude of pinks, reds, mauves or purples as well as white, often with

spotted throats. After flowering, which lasts for about two months, the plant gradually dies back and remains dormant for five or six months.

LIGHT Well-lit position while actively growing but no direct sun-light.

TEMPERATURE When in leaf, a warm position with temperatures around 20°C. When the plant is dormant the tuber should be kept cool but not freezing.

WATERING AND FEEDING Actively growing plants should be kept thoroughly moist but reduce water gradually as the leaves yellow and become dormant. Recommence watering in spring when temperature is around 18°C, encouraging the tuber into growth again. After flowering, feed with a high phosphate fertiliser until the leaves die down in order to build up the tuber for next season's blooms.

SPECIAL CARE If temperatures rise above 24°C the humidity should be increased. If mist-spraying, avoid spraying the plant directly as water will mark the leaves. Repot dormant tubers in spring, keeping the top of the tuber above the soil.

COMMON PROBLEMS Flowering period will be short if light is not bright enough. Rotting may result from poor drainage.

Spathiphyllum

A large-leafed, elegant indoor plant comprising several varieties generally available in spring, but occasionally in summer and autumn, *Spathiphyllum wallisii* is a popular, hardy plant growing to about 30 cm tall. The underground stems give rise to long stalked, glossy green leaves and even longer-stalked flowerheads very similar to lilies. The tiny creamy white flowers are tightly packed around an upright spike (spadix) enclosed by a white spathe which unfolds into a long pointed oval up to 10 cm in length. The colour changes to green over a period of 6-8 weeks. The cultivar 'Mauna Loa' is much larger, almost twice the size of *S. wallisii*.

LIGHT Medium light with no direct sunlight.

TEMPERATURE Normal room temperatures, not less than 12°-14°C in winter. 'Mauna Loa' is not quite as hardy and prefers slightly warmer conditions.

WATERING AND FEEDING When in active growth, water thoroughly but allow the top of the soil to dry before watering again. If temperatures fall, water more sparingly. These rather greedy plants should be fed with liquid or slow-release fertiliser, following the maker's instructions, through spring, summer and autumn.

SPECIAL CARE High humidity is important. Repot annually in spring.

COMMON PROBLEMS Red spider mite may become a pest if the atmosphere is not kept humid. Yellowing foliage may be caused by too much light.

Top ◆ **SPATHIPHYLLUM**
Above ◆ **STREPTOCARPUS**

Streptocarpus

CAPE PRIMROSE

The many cultivars and hybrids of these colourful plants may produce flowers all the year or for at least two or three months, starting in spring. Those most commonly grown have a rosette of slightly puckered leaves and wiry upright stems bearing large, trumpet-shaped flowers with five flaring lobes in white or shades of yellow, pink, red, blue or purple. In some the throats are striped or in a contrasting colour. As some cultivars become dormant for two or three months they are treated as annuals by their owners and discarded when flowering finishes, but, if successfully kept through dormancy, will flower even more freely the following year.

LIGHT Bright when flowering and growing actively, but no direct sunlight. Less light is required when dormant.

TEMPERATURE Normal warm room temperatures will produce year round growth. Temperatures between 7°-13°C will induce a dormant period.

WATERING AND FEEDING Keep the soil moist but allow the top to dry between waterings. Water more sparingly if the plant becomes dormant. Feed with a high phosphate fertiliser, following the maker's instructions, while the plant is growing actively.

SPECIAL CARE Streptocarpus varieties need a humid atmosphere, especially as temperatures rise. A well-ventilated but not draughty position will help avoid mildew. Removing spent flowers will encourage fresh ones. Repot after flowering if roots fill the container.

COMMON PROBLEMS Watch for mealy bugs.

Above ◆ **STROMANTHE SANGUINEA**
Right ◆ **SYNGONIUM PODOPHYLLUM**

Stromanthe

Closely related to prayer plants, the two species of *Stromanthe* are grown indoors for their attractive foliage. The underground stems produce fan-like clusters of spear-shaped long-stalked leaves. In *S. amabilis*, which grows to about 30 cm in height, the leaves are up to 22 cm long, grey-green with a feather design of dark green on the upper surface. The leaves of the much taller *S. sanguinea*, which may reach 45 cm in height, are deep glossy green with a darker feather pattern on the upper surface and blood red below. If produced indoors the flower heads of both species are carried clear of the foliage. In *S. amabilis* the spikes of tightly held bracts and small flowers are white, in *S. sanguinea* the bracts are salmon red.

LIGHT Medium; no direct sunlight.

TEMPERATURE Normal room temperatures not below 15°-16°C in winter.

WATERING AND FEEDING Water thoroughly in spring and summer but allow the top of the soil to dry before watering again. In cool weather water more sparingly. Feed only during the warm months using weak liquid fertiliser.

SPECIAL CARE Provide a well-ventilated but draught-free position. Keep the atmosphere humid in hot dry periods. Wipe the leaves clean with a damp cloth but avoid leaf gloss preparations. Repot in early summer only if the plant fills the pot.

COMMON PROBLEMS Watch for red spider mite if the atmosphere is dry.

Syngonium Podophyllum

ARROWHEAD PLANT

In common with other climbers such as *Monstera* the leaves of the arrowhead plant, *Syngonium podophyllum*, change in shape as the plant matures. When young the shape of the long-stalked, glossy leaves is a simple arrowhead but as the plant matures this changes to one with clearly defined lobes, first three but up to eleven by the time it is mature. There are several varieties with variegated leaves. The arrowhead plant has long climbing or trailing stems which will produce aerial roots if trained up a moisture-holding support. With such a support, the plant becomes more vigorous than it would if the stems were allowed to trail freely.

LIGHT Bright but no direct sunlight.

TEMPERATURE Normal room temperatures, not below 13°-16°C in winter.

WATERING AND FEEDING Water thoroughly in spring and summer but allow the top centimetre or so of soil to dry before watering again. Water more sparingly as temperatures fall. Feed with liquid or slow-release fertiliser, following maker's instructions, during spring and summer.

SPECIAL CARE In warm weather the arrowhead needs a humid atmosphere. Clean the leaves with a damp cloth. Plants may be cut back if they become too large. Repot in spring if roots have filled container.

COMMON PROBLEMS Insufficient light will result in small leaves, and in variegated varieties the leaves tend to lose their variegated colour.

Left ◆ **TILLANDSIA USNEOIDES**
Above ◆ **TOLMIEA MENZIESII**

Tolmiea Menziesii

PIGGY-BACK PLANT/YOUTH ON AGE

With its rosette of long-stalked leaves the piggy-back plant, *Tolmiea menziesii*, is suitable for both pots and hanging baskets. A mature plant may spread about 40 cm in diameter and reach 30 cm in height. The light green hairy leaves are roughly heart-shaped, and are toothed and lobed. The piggy-back plant's distinctive characteristic is the formation of young plantlets at the junction of the leaf and stalk. As the leaf ages, the stalk droops over allowing the plantlet to take root in the soil. If the greenish-brown, insignificant flowers are produced they appear on long upright stems.

LIGHT Medium to bright light.

TEMPERATURE Will accept a wide range of temperatures but not below 7°-10°C.

WATERING AND FEEDING Keep soil moist but not waterlogged during spring, summer and autumn but water more sparingly in winter when the plant should rest. Use liquid or slow-release fertiliser,

Tillandsia Usneoides

SPANISH MOSS/GREY-BEARD

One of the most unusual bromeliads, grown more as a curiosity than for its beauty, the intricate Spanish moss, *Tillandsia usneoides*, is a virtually rootless plant. It does not grow in soil, but clings to a tree for support, taking its nourishment from the atmosphere. The long trailing stems are covered with narrow, scale-like silvery leaves up to 7-8 cm long, which absorb atmospheric moisture. In their native tropical America these fine, thread-like stems make tangled clumps up to 6 m in length. They were once used as a substitute for horse hair in making furniture. The small, yellowish-green fragrant flowers change to blue as they mature but are seldom produced indoors.

LIGHT Bright but no direct sunlight.

TEMPERATURE Normal room temperatures not below 5°C in winter.

WATERING AND FEEDING As all moisture is absorbed through its leaves, mist-spray the plant daily and submerge it in tepid water for 10-15 minutes weekly. No feeding is needed.

SPECIAL CARE As it has no roots Spanish moss should be tied to a piece of bark or cork which can be submerged in water.

COMMON PROBLEMS Drying up through lack of moisture.

following maker's directions, only during active plant growth.

SPECIAL CARE Repot in spring when roots fill the container, or plant young plantlets in fresh soil.

COMMON PROBLEMS Too little light will produce pale foliage and very long stalks.

Trachycarpus Fortunei

WINDMILL PALM/CHUSAN PALM

The windmill palm, *Trachycarpus fortunei*, accepts colder conditions and a wider range of light intensity than many indoor plants. The single trunk is covered with grey fibres and the remnants of old stalks. The dark green fan-shaped leaves are blue-green on the undersides, and the broad, radiating, pleated segments are divided from each other for only half their length. The leaf stalks have marginal spines. Although much taller when growing in the garden, indoor specimens rarely grow more than 2 m tall. Flowers are not usually produced on plants grown inside.

LIGHT Medium to bright with some direct sunlight.

TEMPERATURE Normal room temperatures, as low as 7°C.

WATERING AND FEEDING In spring and summer, water thoroughly but allow the top of the soil to dry before watering again. If temperatures fall water more sparingly. Feed with liquid or slow-release fertiliser, following maker's directions, only when palm is growing actively.

SPECIAL CARE If possible a spell in the garden in summer will improve the palm's general health but avoid putting directly into hot sun from a shaded position. Hose gently to clean the foliage. Repot in spring when roots fill the container.

COMMON PROBLEMS Watch for scale and mealy bugs. Lack of new leaves may be the result of insufficient light.

Tradescantia

INCH PLANT/WANDERING JEW

An easy and prolific plant to grow, *Tradescantia* is similar to Zebrina, also known as wandering Jew, although they differ in botanical details. Both *T. albiflora* and *T. fluminensis* have sprawling, shining stems which look attractive in hanging baskets, although they tend to drop the older leaves quite soon. The glossy green leaves of the inch plant, *T. albiflora*, are pointed, narrow ovals up to 3-4 cm in length and the flowers are small and white. Variegated forms with yellow and green, white, or white and purple striped leaves are more commonly grown. The wandering Jew, *T. fluminensis*, also has white flowers and similar foliage but the undersides of the leaves are purple. There are also variegated forms.

LIGHT Bright light with some cool, direct sunlight.

TEMPERATURE Normal room temperatures, warm rather than cool.

WATERING AND FEEDING Keep the soil thoroughly moist in spring and summer but water much more sparingly in the cool months. Feed with liquid or slow-release fertiliser, following maker's instructions, only when the plant is growing actively.

SPECIAL CARE To keep plants bushy pinch out the tips of new shoots. Plants which have grown too big or leggy may be cut back in spring. Repot when plant roots fill the container or put cuttings in water until roots appear then use these to start afresh.

COMMON PROBLEMS Overwatering will cause rotting. Leggy plants are caused by low levels of light.

Above ◆ **TRADESCANTIA**

Vriesea Splendens

FLAMING SWORD

The leaves of the flaming sword, *Vriesea splendens*, form a loose, open rosette typical of the bromeliads. Up to 35 cm long and 3-5 cm wide they are greyish green with broad cross bands of brownish-purple, more strongly defined on the lower surfaces. In midsummer the central flower spike emerges. It may be as much as 50-60 cm tall, terminating in a flattened, sword-shaped head of brilliant red bracts from which the yellow flowers issue. Other forms need similar conditions.

LIGHT Bright with cool direct sunlight.

TEMPERATURE Normal room temperatures but not less than 12°-14°C in winter.

WATERING AND FEEDING In the warm months keep the rosette filled with fresh water and the soil moist. In winter water more sparingly but do not let the soil dry out completely. Use weak liquid fertiliser when watering from spring to autumn.

SPECIAL CARE Like other bromeliads these plants like humid conditions. When flowering finishes the rosette itself will gradually die but young offshoots should have been formed around the base. These should also be filled when watering. Once the offshoots have developed at least two new leaves the central rosette, which is inclined to become rather smelly, may be cut away. Repot in spring only when roots fill the container. The offshoots may take 3-4 years to flower.

COMMON PROBLEMS Hot sun will yellow the leaves and cold conditions with too much soil moisture may cause rotting.

Washingtonia Filifera

COTTON PALM/DESERT FAN PALM

This hardy palm has a rather open crown and is easily grown indoors in a container. If the old leaf stalks are removed as they die, the trunk remains smooth and pale grey, thickening at the base. The greyish-green fan-shaped leaves, which may be up to 60 cm across, are divided into fine radiating segments with long fine white threads curling between them. The stalks are long and spiny. These are vigorous

Left ◆ **VRIESEA SPLENDENS**
Below ◆ **WASHINGTONIA**

plants and if planted out in the garden will reach 15 m or so in height.

LIGHT Bright with some direct sunlight.

TEMPERATURE Normal room temperatures down to 10°C in winter.

WATERING AND FEEDING Although tolerant of dry conditions the cotton palm is healthier when thoroughly watered during the growing period in the warmer months but needs less water in winter. Use liquid or slow-release fertiliser, following maker's directions, during warmer months.

SPECIAL CARE Although not essential, the cotton palm will respond to humidity in hot dry weather. Repot in spring when roots fill the container, probably only every two or three years.

COMMON PROBLEMS May be attacked by scale and mealy bug.

Zebrina Pendula

WANDERING JEW

Often confused with *Tradescantia* and called by the same common name, *Zebrina pendula* is fast growing and extremely easy to cultivate. A rather sprawling plant with trailing stems, it is often grown in a hanging basket to display the foliage. The narrow oval leaves with pointed tips up to 7 cm long are green and white striped on the upper surfaces and purplish-red below. Clusters of small flowers enclosed in two bracts are purplish-rose on the upper surfaces of the lobes and white below. The varieties differ in foliage colour but require similar growing conditions.

LIGHT Bright with a little cool sunlight.

TEMPERATURE Normal room temperatures preferably warm and not less than 12°C.

WATERING AND FEEDING From spring to autumn water thoroughly then allow the top soil to dry before watering again. In cool conditions water more sparingly. Use liquid or slow-release fertiliser, following maker's instructions, while the plant is growing actively.

SPECIAL CARE In hot, dry weather mist-spray to raise humidity. Foliage colour is best in plants which are kept a little dry. Repot in spring when plant fills the container.

COMMON PROBLEMS Overwatering, especially in cool weather, may cause rotting.

Zygocactus cultivars

CHRISTMAS CACTUS

A Brazilian jungle cactus similar to *Rhipsalidopsis* and *Schlumbergera*, *Zygocactus* has been transferred to *Schlumbergera* by botanists but is still known under its old name by horticulturists pioneering the breeding of cultivars. Like the others it has pendent stems composed of flattened segments, with the single or double flowers carried at the tips. These appear in May and June, roughly equivalent in

Top ◆ **ZEBRINA PENDULA**
Above ◆ **ZYGOCACTUS**

climate to December in the northern hemisphere where the *Zygocactus* is usually known as Christmas cactus. The new hybrids are hardy plants and in some the flowers may last up to fourteen days. The colour range is large with well over a hundred varieties to choose from, including bi-coloured forms. Pinks, mauves, purples, oranges and reds are available, many combined with a pink so pale that it passes as white. A recent cultivar from America is the yellow 'Gold Charm'. See also *Schlumbergera*.

LIGHT Medium light with only cool winter sunlight as with Easter cactus.

TEMPERATURE The Christmas cactus prefers normal room temperatures below 30°C although it will survive 37°C.

WATERING AND FEEDING Keep the soil moist most of the year. In Autumn, to encourage flowering, provide only enough water to prevent the plant wilting. Once flower buds can be seen recommence watering and feeding using liquid or half strength slow-release fertiliser.

SPECIAL CARE As large plants in flower are difficult to transport and the flowers are likely to drop with the change of light and temperature, it is better to buy small plants and grow them on. Repot after flowering if necessary.

COMMON PROBLEMS Change of flower colour may be caused by fertiliser or light intensity. White tends to become pink as it ages.

Glossary

AERIAL ROOTS Roots which grow above the ground, from the stem or branches of a plant, and take in nourishment from the atmosphere.

AXIL The angle between a leaf or leaf-stalk and the stem from which it grows.

BASAL LOBE The division of a leaf nearest to the stalk .

BRACT A modified leaf.

CULTIVAR An abbreviation of 'cultivated variety', describing a variety of a plant which originated under cultivation rather than in the wild, and which, when propagated, retains its distinctive characteristics.

GENUS A group of plants whose flowers, fruits and seeds have sufficient similarity to indicate a common ancestor.

GROW ON To encourage a young plant or a struck cutting to continue to grow.

HYBRID A plant with parents from two different species.

LEAF-DROP OR LEAF-FALL Normally leaves fall from the plant when their life cycle is complete. This may be at the end of one or several years. However, a plant under stress will drop its leaves prematurely.

PINCH BACK To remove new, central buds or shoots from the tops of stems to discourage further upward growth and to encourage side shoots, and therefore denser growth patterns.

ROSETTE A cluster of leaves arranged in a circle around a central growing point, commonly at the base of a plant.

SPATHE A modified leaf which wraps around the central spike of flowers.

SPECIES A group of plants within a genus which has the same distinctive characteristics. Although members of the same species may vary somewhat in form and sometimes in flower colour, seedlings raised from plants of the same species will be similar to their parents. The abbreviation for species, singular, is sp. and the plural form is spp.

SPIKE A long, narrow spike-like cluster of flowers arranged closely along an undivided stem. In a botanical sense each single flower is stalkless.

SPORE The reproductive cells of ferns. Spore case: the structure enclosing the spores.

STRIKE A term used to indicate that cuttings (pieces of a plant placed in the soil) have taken root and begun to grow.

SUCCULENT A plant with fleshy leaves in which water is stored.

SUCKER A shoot springing from the roots of a plant. Some plants develop into clumps when new stems continue to grow from the roots as they spread out.

Details of plant entries

NAMES

The plants are arranged alphabetically according to their botanical (generic or species) classification. In some cases you will find the term 'syn.' and a further botanical name in brackets below the plant name in the title. This refers to the plant's former name, a reflection of the fact that the botanical classification of plants is in constant revision as a result of research and periodic world botanical conferences. Most of the plants in the book also have common names, and the most widely-recognised of these are listed below the plant's botanical name.

There is also the occasional entry where the plant name in the title includes an additional name in inverted commas: for example, Polypodium aureum 'Mandaianum'. This indicates that the plant is a cultivar (see glossary) of the species preceding it in the title.

Within the text, hybrids are indicated by the includion of 'x' within the name: for example, Aechmea x 'Foster's Favourite'.

DESCRIPTION

Each entry contains a physical description of the plant, including foliage, flowers and the height to which it is likely to grow (where applicable), for easy identification and planning purposes. The plant's seasonal changes, such as flowering and dormancy periods, are described. Suitability for pots or hanging baskets is also mentioned where applicable.

CARE OF PLANTS

The book provides vital information on each plant's particular requirements concerning light, temperature, watering and feeding, and each entry includes a 'special care' section detailing other specific requirements such as humidity level, cutting and pinching back stems and branches, repotting, ventilation and other factors.

Index